APPOINTMENTS

WITH GOD

APPOINTMENTS

WITH GOD

*"The LORD gave the word! Great was the
company of those that published it."*
Psalm 68:11

GINA RENAY KIMPTON
GINA RENAY STRUM
GINA RENAY GIPPNER
GINA RENAY WOODS
GINA RENAY MEYER

INTRODUCTION

When I first started working on *Appointments with God*, I needed to bring my words to life, so I reached out to my dear friend Lyndsey Barrett, who had expertly guided my first book, *Onward by Faith: A Mother's Journey to Iraq and Back*, to publication. At the time, she had recently launched her new business, Lyndsey Barrett Brand Co., and wasn't available, so she generously recommended her friend and colleague, Deborah Conrad. Deborah and I instantly connected, not only through our shared passion for creating God-centered books but also through our faith. And it didn't take long for me to realize that I didn't want to hire her as a contractor, but I wanted Deborah to be my publishing partner, and when she agreed the two of us created Onward by Faith Publishing.

Our collaboration transformed *Appointments with God* into a true labor of love. As the Bible says, *"Where two or more are gathered..."*(Matthew 18:20), I know that together, we've created something truly special. Thank you, Deborah, for your exceptional talent, dedication, and spiritual alignment.

This book is a testament to the power of partnership and faith, and at Onward by Faith Publishing we are going to work hard to be more than a publishing company. We want to be your friend. Our commitment is deeply personal, as we walk with faith, knowing that every word we pen is written to uplift and empower you, our future friend.

Onward by Faith,
Gina and Deborah

Soul-stirring!

"*This book is a testament to the power of faith and self-discovery. Through the author's journey, you'll find comfort in knowing that questioning your beliefs is part of the journey to strengthening them. With carefully selected Bible verses and a seamless narrative this book will inspire you to look within and explore a deeper meaning to spirituality.*"

Donna Lyons, Author, News Journalist, iHeart Radio Podcast Host

"*More than simply anecdotal, Appointments With God chronicles Gina Renay Meyer's intimate and enviable relationship with her Creator, Comforter, and Best Friend. It is Gina's contribution to the ongoing, never-ending Book of Acts of the Holy Spirit. God's people who know Him as their Good Shepherd, those He affectionately calls by name, are still experiencing the adventure of a Spirit-guided life, one encounter after another. Gina is one of those. Appointments With God will inspire the pre-believer to believe, provoke the casual believer to envy, and challenge the committed believer to an even closer walk with God. This book could be the beginning of a whole new perspective on life, perhaps just the one you've been looking for.*"

Linda Langley, Transformations Unlimited

"*Appointments With God is the story of one person's journey of faith. From an early age, Gina felt the presence of God in her life. She reached out to Him during a moment of crisis and was answered in an extraordinary way. Thus began a relationship that has evolved over time to where she feels God's influence and wisdom in all the moments of her life. Her story is compelling for anyone who is curious about what it means to have a meaningful spiritual life no matter where they might be in life's journey. Once you start reading Appointments With God, you won't be able to put it down.*"

Deborah Morgan Pardee, Writer

"*Gina's book is inspirational, encouraging readers to listen for God's voice in their daily lives. With heartfelt honesty, Gina shares the ups and downs of her journey, revealing how God's presence guides us every step of the way. One of the book's greatest strengths is its thoughtful integration of Scripture, illuminating God's guidance and wisdom.*"

Anna Low, The Farmer's Daughter

TABLE OF CONTENTS

PROLOGUE

On June 19, 2014, I was lying in bed thinking about the past five decades of my life when I closed my eyes, folded my hands and prayed: *"God, all the appointments we've shared... the questions I've had, and the answers You gave — the good, the bad — tonight I need to know one more answer to one more question: Do You want me to publish our time spent together so others can learn that disappointments in life are nothing more than appointments with You? Or do You want me to keep our appointments hidden deep within my heart? Please let me know and I will do whatever You want. In Jesus' name, YOUR WILL BE DONE. AMEN!"*

A few hours after I prayed, I fell asleep and through a dream God showed me exactly how He wanted me to retell the true stories of how we developed a personal relationship — A friendship — A trust — A love for one another — *"What therefore God has joined together, let not man separate."* Mark 10:9

IN THE BEGINNING...

of one's life God speaks to each of us. He comes to us through His scriptures. *"All Scripture is breathed out by God and profitable for teaching, for reproof, for correction, and for training in righteousness, that the man of God may be complete, equipped for every good work."* 2 Timothy 3:16-17

He shows up within our dreams, *"And in the last days it shall be,' God declares, 'that I will pour out My Spirit on all flesh, and your sons and your daughters shall prophesy, and your young men shall see visions, and your old men shall dream dreams.'"* Acts 2:17

He sends messengers on our daily paths, *"Do not neglect to show hospitality to strangers, for thereby some have entertained angels unawares."* Hebrews 13:2

There are many ways He introduces Himself to each person and once we extend our hand back to Him, then we can hear His voice...

"Jesus said to him, 'I am the way, and the truth, and the life. No one comes to the Father except through Me. If you had known Me, you would have known My Father also. From now on you do know Him and have seen Him.'" John 14:6-7

"And the LORD answered me: 'Write the vision; make it plain on tablets, so he may run who reads it. For still the vision awaits its appointed time; it hastens to the end — it will not lie. If it seems slow, wait for it; it will surely come; it will not delay.'" Habakkuk 2:2-3

"Now the word of the LORD came to me, saying, 'Before I formed you in the womb I knew you, and before you were born I consecrated you; I appointed you a prophet to the nations.' Then I said, 'Ah, Lord GOD! Behold, I do not know how to speak, for I am only a youth.' But the LORD said to me, 'Do not say, "I am only a youth"; for to all to whom I send you, you shall go, and whatever I command you, you shall speak. Do not be afraid of them, for I am with you to deliver you,' declares the LORD. Then the LORD put out His hand and touched my mouth. And the LORD said to me, 'Behold, I have put My words in your mouth.'" Jeremiah 1:4-9

Appointment One

"THERE IS AN APPOINTED TIME FOR EVERYTHING"

"For everything there is a season,
and a time for every matter under Heaven."
Ecclesiastes 3:1

Today I walked toward the Garden of God and found myself standing in front of the rusted gate. I knew what awaited me but wasn't sure what emotions I would find. Today is the day of my harvest... *"For everything there is a season, and a time for every matter under Heaven: a time to be born, and a time to die; a time to plant, and a time to pluck up what is planted."* Ecclesiastes 3:1-2

As I looked beyond the gate, I could see the cherubim waiting for me. But what was I to do? I knew my final hour would arrive, but I honestly thought I had more time. I understood that the moment I walked through the gate there would be no turning back so it was at that moment when I asked God, "Before I walk into Your garden will You please allow me one more glimpse of my life?"

God graciously approved my final request...

Hans Christian Anderson once wrote, *"Every person's life is a fairytale written by God's fingers."* I believe he was right. I was born into the world on June 19, and was given the name, Gina, which defined means, "garden." I was also given the middle name, Renay, which defined means, "reborn." It's interesting how I hardly ever share my last names. I have always believed that first names lead us to where we are going, and last names are extensions of the people from our past.

My parents divorced when I was too young to remember, and my mother remarried when I was four, having two more children. Our family was then complete.

Or was it?

Like many children from divorced families, I saw my father on selected weekends — 132 weekends, to be exact. And each one of them brought the same memories. I always felt as if our visits together were like a reoccurring dream. We seemed to do the same things each time. There was no room for variation or spontaneity. From the moment he picked me up until he brought me home again, everything happened the same way. He would pick me up at 10am every third Saturday, in his blue Ford Mustang. We'd only be in the car for five min-utes and we'd begin to sing, *"You are my sunshine, my only sunshine. You make me happy when skies are grey. You'll never know dear how much I love you. Please don't take my sunshine away."* Then we would sing another song that went something like, *"You better get out with a thump, thump, thump, and don't come back no more..."* and as we'd sing, we'd hit our hands on the dashboard of his car, *"thump, thump, thump."* I don't remember the rest of the words. I do, however; remember that every time we had come to the last *"thump"* in the song my father would reach over, grab me, and I would scream in the excitement of the moment.

I have other memories of how we'd talk and laugh about nothing. Or how we would spend our days hiking in the hills by his mother's house, or our evenings playing poker. I loved playing poker because there was something that connected me to the cards I was holding in my tiny hands. Many moments the decades of absence have erased, but one moment changed my life forever.

I remember the last time I spoke with my father, and the conversation we had. It was just days before my 12th birthday and as he was driving me home there was an unfamiliar silence and my heart knew that I was never going to see him again; so, I turned my eyes towards the passenger window, looked onward to Heaven, and asked him, *"Do you believe there is a God? Do you believe there is a Heaven? And if you do, tell me about it."*

I wasn't sure what he would say or how he would react, but at that moment I needed to hear his answer. I wanted to know if Heaven existed or if this was all there was to life.

"Yes, I believe there is a God, and that Heaven exists. Heaven is where there is no more pain and suffering," he replied.

As I was getting out of his car, he reached into his glove compartment and pulled out a small box that was covered in black velvet. He handed me the box and said, *"It's funny that you would ask me today if I believed in God, because there is an appointed time for everything."* He then leaned over and hugged me. A hug that lasted only a moment, but the scent of his cologne stayed with me for decades. As he drove away, I stood out in my driveway and watched. When I could no longer see his taillights, I opened the box and found inside a pink Cinderella watch.

My father was right. There is an appointed time for everything!

When Gina Kimpton became Gina Strum

Appointment Two

"OPEN YOUR EYES, GINA"

"Be strong and courageous. Do not fear or be in dread of them,
for it is I your God who goes with you. I will not leave you or forsake you.""
Deuteronomy 31:6

My first best friend was Connie Buckelew. She was happy, blond, and beautiful, and the two of us met when we were nine years old. Connie had two brothers, and her parents were still together. When I would go to her house I immediately would run to her refrigerator because every morning when her parents were getting ready to go to work, Connie's father would make her mother coffee, and then bring it to her in a "Love is..." coffee mug. He would then go outside and get the morning newspaper because there was a comic strip that was exactly like the mug called, Love is... It had two naked characters always looking at each other lovingly, and was created by cartoonist, Kim Casali. Casali created the characters from love notes that she had written to her future husband, and they seemed to resonate with others who wanted to share their personal sentiments of love. Each day there would be a new sentiment that Connie's father would cut from the newspaper and place on the refrigerator so that Connie's mother could read it before she went to work. One day there was a sentiment that was attached to a refrigerator

magnet that I have never forgotten. It read: Love is never having to say you're sorry.

Connie and I did everything together.

It was a Friday afternoon (several months after my father stopped coming for our visits) when Connie and I were standing in the commissary line at school and suddenly I began to feel sick to my stomach. It wasn't a familiar sickness, but one that sent me into a panic. I had never felt so many emotions at one time, and without thinking I stepped out of line, grabbed my backpack, and began running...

"GINA. WHERE ARE YOU GOING?" Connie yelled.

"I DON'T KNOW, BUT I CAN'T STAY HERE!"

I ran for what seemed like forever until I arrived at the place where my legs could no longer move, and when my breath became too labored to continue, I stopped. I realized I had run into an empty subdivision, and for a moment, I felt as if I was the only person left on the planet. And it was there where I saw it.

A shiny piece of broken glass was beaming into my eyes. The light was so bright I felt as if it was speaking to me. I then found myself walking towards the glass, picking it up and imagined taking the broken glass and sliding it against my wrist... That's it! I thought. I will take this broken glass and with a single slit of my wrist I will be in Heaven, and then one day I will see my father again.

Walking to find a place to sit, I happened to find an unopened pack of cigarettes — Marlboro Lights, to be exact. The thought then occurred to me, if I start smoking, then maybe (by the end of the day) I could die of asphyxiation. So, with my broken glass and the pack of unopened cigarettes I started to walk towards one of the homes being built and noticed that on the front lawn  there was a Dogwood tree that had yet to be planted and was standing alone within a 3-gallon container. The tree looked inviting so I decided I would sit underneath its small branches until I figured out what I was going to do.

Slit my wrist?

Smoke the cigarettes?

As I sat contemplating my next move, I placed the cigarettes in the container of the tree and then without any thought I took the broken glass within my left hand and as quickly as I could I made two sharp cuts along my right wrist. I then sat and watched my blood drip from my wrist to the dirt. But as some moments happen in life, there was a fear of the unknown and I noticed that my cuts were not deep enough. If I was going to do this right, I would have to take deeper cuts, but then I thought... just because my father believed there was a God, and that Heaven was a real place, did I believe that too?

At that moment I looked up to Heaven and said, *"God, if You truly exist, if You are real, do You take people away from us, so we'll want to come to Heaven to see them again? Because if Heaven is real and unless I get to Heaven, I will never see my father again, and..."*

But before I finished my question, I heard the sound of thunder say, *"I am the Alpha and the Omega, the first and the last, the beginning and the end."* Revelation 22:13

Not knowing where the voice was coming from, I jumped to my feet in fear as it continued... *"'Be strong and courageous. Do not fear or be in dread of them, for it is I your God who goes with you. I will not leave you or forsake you.' (Deuteronomy 31:6)... 'but now is not the time for you to end your life, but the time for you to decide on how your life will end. Now, I want you to close your eyes and pay attention. I want you to remember what you see."*

"Then I saw a great white throne and Him who was seated on it. From His presence earth and sky fled away, and no place was found for them. And I saw the dead, great and small, standing before the throne, and books were opened. Then another book was opened, which is the Book of Life. And the dead were judged by what was written in the books, according to what they had done. And the sea gave up the dead who were in it, Death and Hades gave up the dead who were in them, and they were judged, each one of them, according to what they had done. Then Death and Hades were thrown into the lake of fire. This is the second death, the lake of fire." Revelation 20:11-14

"Open your eyes, Gina. Did you see your name written within My Book of Life?"

Trembling and unable to answer the voice continued... *"No, of course not. That is because you do not know if you believe if I Am Who I say I Am. 'Not everyone who says to Me, "Lord, Lord," will enter the Kingdom of Heaven, but the one who does the will of My Father who is in Heaven.'"* Matthew 7:21

"Your Father? You have a Father in Heaven?" I quickly asked.

"GINA! Listen carefully. The unplanted Dogwood tree that you see is yours. You are to take the tree and plant it in My garden, and then you are to leave My garden until I call for you to return. 'Watch therefore, for you know neither the day nor the hour.' (Matthew 25:13), and when I call you — you will return to the very spot in which you planted your tree. When you arrive, you will see My cherubim waiting for you. You will not speak to him but will make one final decision. The decision will be for you to decide if you believe whether I Am who I say I Am."

"If you believe that I Am who I say I Am, then you will stretch out your right hand and place it on the trunk of your tree and every story of your life will be recorded within the tree and your name will be added within the Book of Life. If you do not believe that I Am who I say I Am, then you will stretch out your left hand and place it on the trunk of the tree and My cherubim will cut down your tree and burn it. Your life will be as if you never existed. You see, My child, you are the only person who can find the answers to the questions you are seeking. No one can find them for you. Do you understand?"

Not able to speak, my thoughts began to wander. Was that voice real? Whose voice was that? Was it God? Was I going insane? So many questions kept circling my head. When I couldn't take another thought, I picked up the tree and began running to Connie's house. I needed to tell her what had just happened.

As I was running, I realized that I had to pass by a Hallmark store to get to Connie's house, so I slowed my run to a walk. As I was walking by, I happened to look through the window and saw a paper wallet and decided that I would go in and purchase it. It would be the perfect place to hide my cigarettes that were still safely positioned within the container of my tree.

Walking through the store I grabbed one of the yellow wallets, and without paying attention, I was still holding my broken glass within my left hand. As I went to reach into my backpack to find my money, I placed the broken glass on the counter and my tree on the floor. The woman behind the counter did not say a word. She simply looked at my wrist (that was still dripping with blood), then using a Kleenex, she grabbed my broken glass from the counter, threw it in the trash and then reached below. When her hand returned to where I could see it, I no longer saw my broken glass, but a beautiful glass angel. She then placed the angel on the counter, and then gently slid the angel over to me. I paid for my bag, and without either of us saying a word I picked up the angel and my tree. As I was walking out the door, I happened to notice the clock on the wall and it confirmed that school was over and Connie would be home, so I ran to her house as quickly as I could. When I arrived at her door, I placed the tree on her porch and walked into her house.

"Connie! Where are you?" The house was silent and as I approached her room, I could see that she was lying on her bed, crying.

"What's wrong?" I asked.

Quickly she turned away from me as if to say, *"Leave me alone."* Grabbing her shoulder, I pulled her back towards me. *"What's wrong? Why are you crying?"*

"I just found out my mother has cancer, and I don't know what to do."

Appointment Three

"IS THERE MORE?"

*"Then the L*ORD *God said, 'Behold, the man has become like one of Us
in knowing good and evil. Now, lest he reach out his hand and take also
of the Tree of Life and eat, and live forever—'"*
Genesis 3:22

It was a Tuesday afternoon when Connie and I had arrived at her home. As we walked into her kitchen to grab a bite to eat, we heard Connie's father say, *"Hey girls. Come back to my bedroom and see who's home from the hospital."*

The two of us immediately smiled and ran down the hallway. When we saw that it was her mother we jumped up on the bed in excitement. But within a moment Connie's mother let out a scream, and because the two of us were only 12, we both jumped off the bed, ran out of the house and kept running until we could run no farther.

That was the last time I ever saw Connie's mother. She passed away a short time afterwards, and now my mother and I were attending her funeral — the first funeral I had ever attended so I had no idea what to expect. My past months had been such a blur. I still had not told anyone about my Dogwood tree, and I had come to the opinion that there was no point in planting it. My best friend had just lost

her mother so if there was a God, why would He allow anyone to suffer that much?

"Connie," I said, *"I'm here if you need anything."*

"I know, Gina. I have to go sit with my family. I'll talk to you later."

Connie went and sat with her family. I went and sat with my mother. While the pastor was officiating, all I could do was stare at Connie. The once happy, beautiful, blond girl was now so sad, and there was nothing I could do to help her. When the service was over the pastor shared that the family would be attending the grave site and that everyone else could head down to the reception. As my mother and I were following the crowd I told her that I had forgotten something in the car. When she was out of my sight, I bolted up to the final resting place of Connie's mother and hid behind a tree.

When the moment of Connie's life changed, and her mother was placed in the ground, everyone left, and that was when the pastor noticed me hiding and motioned for me to come to him. Not wanting to move I stood behind the tree, so he came to me.

"Did you find comfort standing behind the tree?" he asked.

"What?"

"Did you find the comfort you were seeking by standing behind the tree?" he asked again.

"I guess so. Why?"

"Because you were told to go to the reception, but you disobeyed and hid behind the tree. Do you know who Adam and Eve are?"

"You mean the Adam and Eve from the Bible?"

"Yes." He then smiled as he opened his Bible to Genesis and began to read...

"And the LORD God planted a garden in Eden, in the east, and there He put the man whom He had formed. And out of the ground the LORD God made to spring up every tree that is pleasant to the sight and good for food. The Tree of Life was in the midst of the garden, and the Tree of the Knowledge of Good and Evil." Genesis 2:8-9

Then, turning toward me, he pointed his finger to the Bible, as if to show me that what he was reading was true, *"Look here,"* he said. *"God created everything. He created the earth, the sky, the stars, the water, the very air we breathe, men, women, and here's where He's talking to Adam."* Pulling the Bible towards him, he continued... *"And the LORD God commanded the man, saying, 'You may surely eat of every tree of the garden, but of the tree of the Knowledge of Good and Evil you shall not eat, for in the day that you eat of it you shall surely die.' Then the LORD God said, 'It is not good that the man should be alone; I will make him a helper fit for him.' Now out of the ground the LORD God had formed every beast of the field and every bird of the heavens and brought them to the man to see what he would call them. And whatever the man called every living creature, that was its name."* Genesis 2:16-19 *"So the LORD God caused a deep sleep to fall upon the man, and while he slept took one of his ribs and closed up its place with flesh. And the rib that the LORD God had taken from the man He made into a woman and brought her to the man."* Genesis 2:21-22 *"And the man and his wife were both naked and were not ashamed."* Genesis 2:25

"Now, here's where the story gets good," he said. *"Now the serpent was more crafty than any other beast of the field that the LORD God had made. He said to the woman, 'Did God actually say, "You shall not eat of any tree in the garden"?' And the woman said to the serpent, 'We may eat of the fruit of the trees in the garden, but God said, "You shall not eat of the fruit of the tree that is in the midst of the garden, neither shall you touch it, lest you die."' But the serpent said to the woman, 'You will not surely die. For God knows that when you eat of it your eyes will be opened, and you will be like God, knowing good and evil.'"* Genesis 3:1-5

"Wait!" I said, interrupting him. *"Why are you reading this to me?"*

But he continued, *"So when the woman saw that the tree was good for food, and that it was a delight to the eyes, and that the tree was to be desired to make one wise, she took of its fruit and ate, and she also gave some to her husband who was with her, and he ate. Then the eyes of both were opened, and they knew that they were naked. And they sewed fig leaves together and made themselves loincloths. And they heard the sound of the LORD God walking in the garden in the cool of the day, and the man and his wife hid themselves from the presence of the LORD God among the trees of the garden. But the LORD God called to the man and said to him, 'Where are you?'*

And he said, 'I heard the sound of You in the garden, and I was afraid, because I was naked, and I hid myself.' He said, 'Who told you that you were naked? Have you eaten of the tree of which I commanded you not to eat?'" Genesis 3:6-11

"Stop reading this!" I said. *"Why are you telling me this story?"*

"Because you hid behind the tree. I told everyone to go to the reception, but you disobeyed my request and because you knew it was wrong you hid from my presence, and when you were caught, I called you, but you neglected to come to me and I had to come to you, but more importantly... because God put it on my heart to read His message to you. Now, before we go to the reception, I have one more verse God wants me to read, and it will be for you to figure out what it means." Then finding his place within his Bible he concluded.

"Then the LORD *God said, 'Behold, the man has become like one of Us in knowing good and evil. Now, lest he reach out his hand and take also of the Tree of Life and eat, and live forever—'"* Genesis 3:22

When the pastor seemed to have read enough, he closed his Bible, smiled, and as he started to walk away, I yelled, *"IS THERE MORE?"*

"What?" he asked.

"Is there more to where you read, lest he stretch out his hand and take from the Tree of Life?"

The pastor walked back towards me and without opening his Bible he recited, *"...therefore the* LORD *God sent him out from the garden of Eden to work the ground from which he was taken. He drove out the man, and at the east of the garden of Eden He placed the cherubim and a flaming sword that turned every way to guard the way to the Tree of Life."* Genesis 3:23-24

"Wait! What is a cherubim?" I asked.

"The guardian of God."

Appointment Four

"BORN WITH WISDOM, DIED WITH GRACE"

"Therefore, stay awake, for you do not know on what day your Lord is coming."
Matthew 24:42

As the pastor walked down to the reception, I stood back for a moment to absorb all that he had shared, and it was then when I looked around the cemetery and noticed something. Not understanding what I was seeing I began to move in a slow circle and with each step I took I no longer noticed all the names written on stones that lay above the grass. But I noticed all the beautiful trees that were planted within the garden and then it dawned on me... If man was created from dirt... If the only way to get to Heaven is to die, then the Garden of God must lie within the cemetery.

As my mother and I were driving home my heart began to race and I knew that I had to think of a way to get my tree planted within the cemetery, so I looked over to her and said, *"Mom, I have an idea. I noticed there were lots of trees planted at the cemetery. I was wondering if I could plant a tree there in memory of Connie's mother. I know that we brought flowers, but I think it would be nice to plant a tree."*

"Gina, what are you talking about? You can't just plant a tree at the cemetery if you're not family."

"What if I get permission? Can I plant one then?"

"If you get permission, but only if you get permission. Do you understand me? And where are you going to get a tree?"

Not knowing how to answer her question I just smiled and said, *"I'll figure out something."*

A few weeks went by, and I still hadn't asked permission from Connie's family. I had no idea how to ask, so I told my mom I was going to walk over to a friend's house, and I would be home within a few hours. When she agreed, I snuck into our back yard and grabbed my Dogwood tree that I had hidden behind a large bush. When I saw that no one was out on our street I scurried to the corner and waited for the bus. The cemetery was only a few blocks away from the library so all I had to do was get there and then I would figure out what to do next.

As I arrived at the cemetery, I noticed that no one was outside. A few parked cars stood by, but all was quiet. I walked to the far east corner and found where I would plant my tree. It was perfect. Situated behind a rusted gate I saw a dilapidated headstone. I knew that no one had been by in decades, so I opened the rusted gate and when I was within reaching distance to the headstone I bent down and brushed off the dirt that had cemented itself within the writing and read:

Zophyah Grace

Born with Wisdom – Died with Grace

Aged 4,380 days

Born 1863 – Died 1875

As I stood up, I couldn't help but wonder if she was trying to tell me something from beyond her grave. She was 12 when she had died, and I too was 12. She was born with wisdom and died with grace. I was trying to find wisdom and had no idea how dying could be graceful.

But since I felt comfortable that no one would be by anytime soon to leave flowers, I decided I would plant my tree within the rusted gate and be done with it, and that's when I realized that I had forgotten to bring a shovel. Not knowing what to do I quietly said, *"God, I don't know if you're real, but I brought the tree, and now I can't plant it. I don't have a shovel."*

"Hello! Can I help you?" A voice said.

I turned around and there was a man sitting in a golf cart. *"Um... No... I'm okay... I just... Um..."*

"Do you need help planting that tree?" he asked.

"Um... No... I'm okay..."

Silently, the man got out of the golf cart, reached into the back and pulling out a shovel he said, *"I know how hard it is when we lose someone from our family, and we want to make sure that we plant something in their memory. By the looks of her grave this tree will bring life back to His garden. Here. Let me dig the hole for you and then I will leave you so you can plant your tree."* Without saying another word, the man dug my hole and when it was deep enough, he smiled, got back in his golf cart and drove away.

When the man was out of sight, I took my Dogwood tree and placed it within the hole, and as I bent down to begin covering its roots with dirt I happened to look beyond the rusted gate and I could see where Connie's mother was buried. It was here where I learned that Connie's father was right to tell her mother every single day that he loved her, because it's true, Love is never having to say you're sorry!

Then as I finished placing the last bit of dirt around my tree I took a deep breath, closed my eyes and again my heart heard *"The unplanted Dogwood tree that you see is yours. You are to take the tree and plant it in My garden, and then you are to leave My garden until I call for you to return. 'Watch therefore, for you know neither the day nor the hour.' (Matthew 25:13), and when I call you — you will return to the very spot in which you planted your tree. When you arrive, you will see My cherubim waiting for you. You will not speak to him but will make one final decision. The decision will be for you to decide if you believe whether I Am who I say I Am. If you believe that I Am who I say I Am, then you will stretch out your right hand and place it on the trunk of your tree and every story of your life will be recorded within the tree and your name will be added within the Book of Life. If you do not believe that I Am who I say I Am, then you will stretch out your left hand and place it on the trunk of the tree and My cherubim will cut down your tree and burn it. Your life will be as if you never existed. You see, My child, you are the only person who can find the answers to the questions you are seeking. No one can find them for you. Do you understand?"*

When I opened my eyes, I looked down and noticed the wind was blowing the leaves of my tree against Zophyah's headstone. The sound of the leaves made me feel as if God was tapping His fingers on a table as if He were waiting for my answer to His question, *"Do you understand?"*

I quietly took two steps backwards, closed the rusted gate, and as I turned to walk onward by faith, I said, *"Yes. I understand."*

I never looked back.

Appointment Five

"I WILL GIVE YOU MY LIFE FOR A LIFE"

"You will make your prayer to Him, and He will hear you,
and you will pay your vows."
Job 22:27

It was Friday, my last day of 8th grade. Connie and I walked home from school and were excited at the thought of summer. The two of us chatted the whole way home about all the things we'd do: go to the beach and the mall, babysit, earn lots of money, bake cookies and eat them. Our ideas of summer were endless, and we were happy, because even though both of us were missing someone we loved, we both were smiling and giggling at the thought of summer.

As we were walking home, we each posed for what the world now calls a "selfie," and when we were done I said, *"Bye, Connie. I'll see you in a bit. I'm going to run home and drop off my stuff."*

"Okay. See you soon!"

I ran home and when I entered the house my mother was waiting for me at the kitchen table. *"Did you have a good day?"*

"Yes. I can't wait for summer," I said.

"Gina, there's something I need to talk to you about, but I didn't want to tell you until school was over."

"What is it, mom?"

"We're moving. We were supposed to move months ago, but I didn't want to take you out of school."

"What do you mean? I can't move! All my friends are here. Connie needs us!" I said through my tears.

"I know. I don't want to move either, but your stepfather drives too far to work each day and it's the way it is. We'll be moving the week before you start high school, so you'll have the summer to be with your friends. I don't want to hear any more about this."

"What about my tree?" I asked.

"What tree? What are you talking about?"

"The tree I planted at the... Oh never mind. I'm not supposed to go see it again until — It doesn't matter anymore. Nothing matters because nothing in life is ever good!"

Summer ended and my life changed. I started high school and my mother had to go back to work. As the oldest, the job of "helper" immediately went to me. I would arrive home from school and be the caretaker of two children. I loved the job, and within months I had established a clientele of parents who weekly would hire me to watch their children. I was raised during the generation before children could make choices. A parent told you to do something and you did it.

On the weekends though, when my parents were home, I played soccer. I loved the game. Every weekend I would get on my bike and head to the field. I also ran the concession stand, so I would get there early, turn on the coffee, heat up the hot dogs and then I would open the window and yell, "WINDOW'S OPEN! COME AND GET IT!"

Part of my pay was I could eat all the candy my stomach could handle. I loved the responsibility, but mostly I loved the free candy.

It was a Saturday and we had played our last game of the season when the coach asked if I would like to come back on Sunday and help him clean out the concession stand. I agreed.

On Sunday (as I was riding my bike toward the field) I saw a little white church on the left-hand side of the street. As I rode past, I watched families going inside. Before I knew it, I was at the field, and we managed to clean up the concession stand rather quickly.

Heading home, I rode on the right-hand side of the street and noticed the little white church again. As I got closer I could see cars pulling into the parking lot and I decided I would lay my bike on the grass and go inside.

As I walked in I saw that the little white church was full, so I went and sat in the back to listen. I did not understand a word of what the man in the purple robe was saying, but I knew that my soul liked it. It was the first time that I had walked into a room where I felt like I belonged.

After the service was over, I went home. Not saying where I had been, (not because my parents would have cared) but because I was trying to figure out "where" that was. Did all those people really believe there was a God? Who was that Jesus the man in the purple robe was talking about? What was the Holy Spirit? Was He talking about the voice who gave me the tree? Was I insane?

The following Saturday I was staying the night at my friend Kris Johnson's house when she asked, *"Gina, do you want to come to church with me tomorrow? We go to Redeemer Lutheran Church down the street."*

"You do? I was there last week. I didn't see you."

"We go to the early service, not the late one. Which one did you go to?"

"The late one."

"Well, it doesn't matter. Do you want to go tomorrow or not? If you do, you'll have to go home early and put on a dress or something nice. We have to dress nice."

"Kris, do you think that whole God, Jesus, Holy Spirit thing is a little crazy?"

"No, I don't. Do you want to go or not?"

The next morning, I woke up early, rushed home, changed into fresh clothes, and began a journey that would last 104 Sundays at the little white church. I also became the daycare provider and secretary to the board of directors. And while I was searching for answers about God, Jesus, and the Holy Spirit, I was also learning about how to navigate my own struggles, and I was trying to find my place in the world, to make sense of my own story, and to understand what it meant to truly live.

Then that Sunday arrived. My 105th Sunday to be exact, where I heard the pastor reading from 1 John 2:18-27...

"Children, it is the last hour, and as you have heard that antichrist is coming, so now many antichrists have come. Therefore we know that it is the last hour. They went out from us, but they were not of us; for if they had been of us, they would have continued with us. But they went out, that it might become plain that they all are not of us. But you have been anointed by the Holy One, and you all have knowledge. I write to you, not because you do not know the truth, but because you know it, and because no lie is of the truth. Who is the liar but he who denies that Jesus is the Christ? This is the antichrist, he who denies the Father and the Son. No one who denies the Son has the Father. Whoever confesses the Son has the Father also. Let what you heard from the beginning abide in you. If what you heard from the beginning abides in you, then you too will abide in the Son and in the Father. And this is the promise that He made to us — eternal life.

I write these things to you about those who are trying to deceive you. But the anointing that you received from Him abides in you, and you have no need that anyone should teach you. But as His anointing teaches you about everything, and is true, and is no lie — just as it has taught you, abide in Him."

When the pastor finished, I couldn't breathe. Immediately I bowed my head and quietly asked, *"Was that You who gave me the tree or was that the one the pastor calls the antichrist?"*

I then took a deep breath and whispered, *"Okay. If You're the one true God, The voice I heard the day when I was going to end my life... The one who gave me the tree... If You are Him, then I want to make a deal with You. I am going to promise You something that only You would know. I promise You that if You forgive me for wanting to have sex, and for having sex before I am married: if You keep me from getting pregnant before I am married, I PROMISE YOU... I will give You my life for a life. DEAL!"*

As I walked out of the church, I immediately wondered why I chose to ask Him not to get pregnant until I was married over asking him for something else. Anything else, but I didn't, and my life continued onward.

Appointment Six

"I WONDER IF ANYONE IS TRULY EVER READY TO LEAVE THE LIFE THEY KNOW FOR THE LIFE THEY'VE NEVER MET"

"But because of the temptation to sexual immorality,
each man should have his own wife and each woman her own husband."
1 Corinthians 7:2

It was Saturday, the day I was to be married. Within hours I would be walking down the aisle of the little white church I walked into years before. I should have been more excited, but I felt tired, anxious, but at least I felt. I wasn't sure if either one of us were doing this for the right reason. Did I understand love? Did I love him like that? Did he understand love? Did he love me like that? What was the "like that" I was looking for?

Yes. I loved being with him. He was handsome, smart, a good worker... but we fought. We fought all the time. But there was that "something" that would always bring us back together, and since I had no idea what to do about my emotions, I sat down and began to write to myself.

Today is Saturday and within a few hours I will be his Mrs.

What are we doing?

I want my mother.

I immediately put down my pen, grabbed a cigarette and asked my mom to come and sit outside with me. Yes, that habit I had picked up years before had stayed with me. It wasn't the same pack, but just the same, I always wondered if it was the reason I continued to smoke.

As the two of us were sitting outside I couldn't help but share my emotions, *"Mom, I have to say something. My body feels as if I'm pregnant. I don't get it. I used two forms of birth control. I haven't missed my cycle, but there's something inside me that's telling me differently."*

"Gina, it's probably just the stress of getting married. Even though it's supposed to be the best day of your life, it's also one of the most stressful. Just go and enjoy your today and tomorrow you'll feel better."

I put out the cigarette, walked back into my bedroom and continued writing...

Looking around my room I see all my plants (that I will come back and retrieve). I see my bedroom set that my parents bought me when I turned 16. I still love the gift. I see my brown, earth-toned bedspread, and valance that my mother made for me. I see a picture of my grandmother and my aunt. How I love that photograph. I see my record player that still has my Carpenters album on it. I see my telephone with a sticker that reads: I love David. (Oops. Never took that off). I won't be taking that phone with me. I see my dog lying on the bed. I won't be taking him with me either. He's the family dog, and... oh, where is the Kleenex when I need one? I see a room filled with memories — all my friends who stayed the night, to late-chats on the phone, and pulling all-nighters studying. My sister and brother... who will watch over them? This is why I never moved out after graduation. I miss them already. This moment is depressing the hell out of me. They are going to grow up without me.

When Gina Strum became Gina Gippner

Well, time to go, Gina. Are you ready?

I wonder if anyone is truly ever ready to leave the life they know for the life they've never met?

Appointment Seven

"WHAT ARE YOU HERE FOR?"

"And if we know that He hears us in whatever we ask,
we know that we have the requests that we have asked of Him."
1 John 5:15

It was Sunday and I was married. I didn't think I would make it through the service. Pastor Larave stopped the service, grabbed my hands, and asked me if I was okay. I kept looking at the cross, wondering: If God was real... where was He? I was hoping He was in the room and would give me a sign or a piece of His peace that I so desperately needed.

It was Monday when my husband and I arrived in Hawaii for our honeymoon. How I hated to fly. I was fine at first, but once we passed the coast of San Francisco, and I could no longer see the land, I wanted the pilot to turn around and take me home. I wasn't feeling well and by the time we landed all I wanted to do was go to our hotel room and fall asleep, and that's exactly what I did.

It was Tuesday. Waking up, I felt as if something inside me was trying to break free. Instead of complaining, I got up and dressed so my husband and I could go see the sights. While we were having breakfast, I couldn't eat so we went back to the hotel where I slept for another few hours. When I awoke the pain was so bad, I went to the hotel physician. She ran a few tests and told me to come back at 10am the following day.

It was Wednesday at 10:00am when I found myself sitting in a hotel examining room. As I was waiting, I couldn't help but wonder what news the doctor would walk through the door with and within minutes the door flung open with a stern voice saying, *"I've got good news and bad news. Which news do you want first?"*

"The good news, please."

"Well, the good news is you have a bladder infection, and the bad news is you're pregnant. We think it might be a tubular pregnancy. We need you to go to the hospital right now and get it checked. If so, you'll have to terminate the pregnancy before you fly home."

My heart stopped.

It was Thursday and I found myself sitting in the hospital waiting... *"Well, we've got your results, and it looks as if your baby is going to be okay, but you may have a difficult pregnancy so if you don't want to keep the child, you'll have to have an abortion soon. You're nearly four months pregnant!"*

I knew I was pregnant, but for the life of me I couldn't figure out how. With two forms of birth control, and never missing a cycle, how could I be pregnant and that far along?

How quickly days recycle themselves, we were back home, and it was Saturday again. My parents had come to the airport to pick us up and while my mother and I were side-by-side walking through the corridor I said, *"Remember last week when I told you I thought I was pregnant?"*

"Yes."

"Well, I am. I'm nearly four months along and they say it could be a difficult pregnancy."

"Oh, Gina. What are you going to do?" she asked. *"You just got married. You have a great job. Well, don't worry about it. I'll take care of it. I want you to go and speak to your doctor."*

Silence fell within the car as we drove home from the airport.

It was Wednesday, and as promised, my mother made an appointment for me to go and see my doctor. I had seen Dr. Fingerly, weekly for nearly six years.

I was highly allergic to many things so two days a week I would show up at his office for my allergy shots. During my younger years, before I owned a car, I would walk with my brother and sister to his office, get my shot, and the three of us would walk home. If there was ever a doctor that I loved and respected, it would be him.

"Gina, I hear that you're going to have a baby," he said. *"You must be so excited!"*

Then through my tears I replied, *"I'm not sure what to do. Everyone thinks I should..."* But quickly my doctor interrupted, *"Gina, I've known you for years. Always coming in to get your allergy shots, and when you came, you rarely came alone. You always had your sister and brother with you. You love children. You're married now. You have a good job. A home. What are you here for?"*

I wanted to say, *"I'm here because of the pressure. Everyone keeps telling me what I should or shouldn't do and it's not about what everyone else thinks!!! When it comes to a woman and her child a person's first response should be to say, 'Congratulations!!!' Babies are innocent. Babies are beautiful. Babies are not mistakes but are sometimes born into the world because they are unplanned, not because they are unwanted."*

But I didn't say a thing. I simply cried, grabbed my purse, ran out the door and into my car. I couldn't breathe, and all I wanted to do was find my way home, but when I got to the boulevard, I found they had closed the road. Instead of taking my normal left, I had to take a right. Then a left. Then another left. As I was driving, tears streamed down my face, making it hard for me to see. When I found myself at a stop sign, I turned my head to the left, and noticed a young boy sitting in the passenger seat of his mother's car and he was pointing at me. I didn't want him to see my mascara-stained face, so I immediately turned my head to the right, and that is when I saw it.

THE CROSS!

Without paying attention I had driven down the road to where my little white church was, and I immediately turned right into the parking lot, got out of my car, and remembered. I remembered the deal I had made with God. The promise that only He knew about...

"Okay. If You're the one true God, The voice I heard the day when I was going to end my life... The one who gave me the tree... If You are Him, then I want to make a deal with You. I am going to promise You something that only You would know. I promise You that if You forgive me for wanting to have sex, and for having sex before I am married: if You keep me from getting pregnant before I am married, I PROMISE YOU... I will give You my life for a life. DEAL!"

October 12 was a Wednesday, the day that I fell on my knees in the church parking lot, and through my tears, I realized that while I got pregnant before I was married, God waited to reveal my pregnancy until after. At that moment I gave my life to God and even though I didn't personally know Him, I knew that I would spend the rest of my life trying to.

Appointment Eight

"SHE WILL STOP AT NOTHING TO FIND WISDOM"

"For the promise is for you and for your children and for all who are far off, everyone whom the Lord our God calls to Himself."

Acts 2:39

It was on a Thursday evening that my son, Glenn James, was born. He came into the world on April 19th, weighing 6 lbs. 12.5 oz., and he was perfect. I remember the moment when Dr. Toomer placed him in my arms and my heart beat in a way that I never wanted it to stop. I felt love, peace, joy, happiness, excitement, but then when the nurse took him out of my arms, that was the moment when I first felt fear, and for a moment I couldn't breathe.

A few weeks after Glenn was born, I called, Pastor Larave, the man I used to call, "The man in the purple robe," and asked him to come over so he could meet my son. There seemed to be an urgency for me to introduce them. Maybe because of the promise that I made to God that day. My life for a life, or maybe it was more than that. Maybe it was because I wanted to introduce him to the child that God had given me.

Me!

The woman who bargained with Him. The woman who tested Him. The woman who was searching but wasn't sure whom she was searching for. God had given me a child, and because of my son, that was the moment when I began to understand the connection between God and His Son, Jesus.

Yes, I wanted my pastor to meet the child born to me and when his knock at the door arrived, I couldn't wait to let him in.

"Gina, what a beautiful baby God has blessed you with," he said. *"Have you thought about when you're going to have him baptized?"*

"Baptized?"

"Yes, you know. Baptized. I know you've read the Gospel of Matthew where Jesus tells us to, 'Go therefore and make disciples of all nations, baptizing them in the name of the Father and of the Son and of the Holy Spirit,'" (28:19) he said.

"I haven't thought that far in advance. He's only 14 days old. I'll have to talk with my husband when he gets home."

Pastor Larave left and a few hours later my husband returned home from work. *"How was your day?"* he asked. I proceeded to tell him about the events that unfolded and that I was supposed to baptize Glenn, but truth-be-told... I didn't even know what that was. I had gone to church for years and never once did I see anyone get baptized. I read about it in the New Testament, never understanding the who, when, where, or why any one person truly needed to be dunked in water.

"Well, I can help you with this decision," my husband said. *"Absolutely not will our son be baptized. Glenn will only be baptized when he chooses to be baptized. It's not the church's choice for a person to have a relationship with God. It's between God and each person. Glenn will have to make his own decision when he's old enough to understand the decision he's making. Do you understand?"*

No, I didn't understand, but a week later I left my little white church, and we found another church. I didn't leave my church because I didn't love Pastor Larave or the people who attended. I left because I needed to understand the God I was trying to know, and I needed a place where I could find what I was looking for. A mother's love is a funny thing. It changes everything. Fear is a funny thing. It changes everything. And, when a mother loves her child so much to where she's afraid of giving her child wrong council she will stop at nothing to find wisdom.

Appointment Nine

"THE FIVE CROWNS"

"For what is our hope or joy or crown of boasting before
our Lord Jesus at His coming? Is it not you?"
1 Thessalonians 2:19

Two years had passed from the time we had left my little white church to the Sunday when I heard Pastor Ron ask, *"Gina, are you ready to be baptized?"*

Nodding, I walked into a tub of water and heard, *"Brothers and sisters in the Lord. Today we stand before you with a woman who is dedicating her life to Christ, and I would like her to take a few moments to tell us why she has decided to make her commitment to Jesus Christ as her Lord and Savior. Here you go, Gina. Talk to us!"*

Pausing for a moment, I looked over at the congregation and noticed every eye was upon me thinking, what will she say?

What I wanted to say was, *"Ladies and gentlemen of the congregation, I am here today because of the child that I carry within my womb. As you can see, I am eight months pregnant with my second child, a daughter. And, because I wasn't 'allowed' to baptize my son, and even more so because I'm still confused as to whether I should have baptized him... Now, I've decided that I'm going to make sure that this child gets baptized through me, and that she's born into this world with forgiveness of anything she will do after she enters this world. I want to ensure a safe passage for my daughter into this world and onward to the next."*

But no. That's not what I said. I stood up there in silence and for a moment I could hear my mother's voice in my head saying, *"Why are you getting baptized? You were baptized Catholic as a baby."* Then I started to think how I grew up Lutheran... and today I was getting baptized as a Baptist. It felt like a joke... A Catholic, Lutheran, and Baptist walk into a bar and ask for a cup of water. Who gets served first?

When my thoughts ended, I shared my heart, and then Pastor Ron placed his arm behind my back, and as he gently pulled me into the water he said, *"I baptize you in the name of the Father, Son, and of the Holy Spirit."* As he pulled me up, I wiped the water from my eyes and without thinking I began to wave at everyone. For some reason I felt as if I had just been crowned Miss America, and the parade wave seemed appropriate.

When the church service was over a woman walked up to me and asked if I felt different.

"You know, I do! But not in the way that I thought I would feel. I felt as if I won a Miss America Contest. I felt like a crown was placed on my head and..." *"Oh Gina,"* she interrupted, *"I've never heard anyone describe it like that, but it's like what they call, The Five Crowns. Look it up."*

It was a Thursday when I made an appointment to visit Pastor Lareva. I always seemed to call on him when I needed a friend. I wanted to ask him about the Five Crowns and within the simplicity of our conversation he said, *"I'll be back in a bit."* When he returned, he handed me an envelope that was sealed and said, *"Here you go."*

When I arrived home, I opened the envelope and found he had handwritten the answer to my question with red ink and it read:

1) The Crown of Life

"Blessed is the man who remains steadfast under trial, for when he has stood the test he will receive the crown of life, which God has promised to those who love Him." James 1:12

"Do not fear what you are about to suffer. Behold, the devil is about to throw some of you into prison, that you may be tested, and for ten days you will have trib-

ulation. *Be faithful unto death, and I will give you the crown of life.*" Revelation 2:10

2) The Incorruptible Crown

"*Every athlete exercises self-control in all things. They do it to receive a perishable wreath, but we an imperishable.*" 1 Corinthians 9:25

3) The Crown of Righteousness

"*Henceforth there is laid up for me the crown of righteousness, which the Lord, the righteous judge, will award to me on that day, and not only to me but also to all who have loved His appearing.*" 2 Timothy 4:8

4) The Crown of Glory

"*And when the chief Shepherd appears, you will receive the unfading crown of glory.*" 1 Peter 5:4

5) The Crown of Exaltation

"*For what is our hope or joy or crown of boasting before our Lord Jesus at His coming? Is it not you?*" 1 Thessalonians 2:19

"*Therefore, my brothers, whom I love and long for, my joy and crown, stand firm thus in the Lord, my beloved.*" Philippians 4:1

When I finished reading my first thought was, Huh? But then I decided to grab my dictionary and I looked up the word crown because that seemed like the best place to start.

Crown: (noun) a royal headdress or cap of sovereignty.

Then I looked up the word, sovereignty: (noun) supreme excellence or an example of it.

As I was reading these definitions my heart began to race because I knew that when I got baptized my relationship with God had changed. It also meant that I could no longer just say that I believed there was a God. I would have to try and live my life as if I was wearing a crown that would be fitting for the one who had placed it on my head.

May 28th was a Wednesday when my daughter, Heidi Lynn, entered the world. She was perfect in every way, but there was something different about her. She was born quickly with no time for anyone to prepare for her arrival and when she was born, she came out with a voice that travelled through the hallways and beyond. On the evening of her first day, the nurse brought her to me and placed her in my arms and that was the moment when I understood the meaning of the Five Crowns and the blessings that my children will be able to receive when they are grown if they choose to receive their crown.

The blessing is... when they are old enough to understand... when they have grown in the Lord, then they too can decide if they want to replace their "g" within the word grown for their "c" and it will be there where they will be able receive their crown.

I understood what my husband was talking about. Within the simplicity of choices, each person must be old enough to understand the decision that we are making or someone else will make it for us, and like God once told me the day He gave me my tree... *"You see, My child, you are the only person who can find the answers to the questions you are seeking. No one can find them for you. Do you understand?"*

"Yes! I do!"

APPOINTMENT TEN

"THIRD TIME'S A CHARM"

"May the God of hope fill you with all joy
and peace as you trust in Him."
Romans 15:13a

It was Tuesday, September 20th, when God blessed me with the birth of my last child. My daughter, Shae Marie, arrived early in the morning with the cord wrapped around her neck. She wasn't immediately placed in my arms because Dr. Toomer had to help her find her breath.

A few hours later the nurse brought her into my hospital room and positioned her securely in my arms. I felt so much joy that she had survived her birth, but I also felt sadness because I knew that I would never want to put her down. There's something about knowing how fragile life is that it made me want to hold on to her forever — but forever is a funny thing. It only lasts for a moment, and before I knew it, I was placing her in her car seat, and off we drove to introduce her to her brother and sister.

It was love at first sight.

Then six days later I was sitting on the couch, and Shae was in her bassinet. To the left of Shae was her brother, Glenn, and to the right of her was her sister, Heidi, so at that moment I grabbed a piece of paper and wrote...

At this moment in time, Shae is six days old. When I think that she is my last child, I can't help but cry. I wanted to have six children, but it seems my body will only allow me to have three. I now agree. Third time's a charm. Shae was born with the cord wrapped around her neck and because of that, I can't bear to place her where I can't see her. I need to watch her breathe.

I want to try and describe how I feel at this moment. There was a time when I didn't understand what it felt like to feel love. But now (because of you three) I know what it's like to love so much that my heart is full. I can't describe the fullness of love, but I do know this... I'm going to place this note where it might one day be found. The message I want you three to find is this... *"May the God of hope fill you with all joy and peace as you trust in Him."* Romans 15:13, because trusting in God is what will bring you true joy and peace.

Nothing else ever will.

Appointment Eleven

"I CONFESS"

"...because, if you confess with your mouth that Jesus is Lord and
believe in your heart that God raised Him from the dead, you will be saved."
Romans 10:9

It was a Sunday that I never wanted to forget, so I grabbed my notebook and my favorite pen and began to scribe...

Many years ago, soon after my daughter, Heidi, was born, I became very ill. Every six months or so, I found myself either in the hospital having surgery or recovering from whatever illness I happened to contract. With each hospital stay I seemed to bring home a memory, but on one hospital stay I brought home a promise that I needed to inscribe, because I never want to forget or change the moment that changed my life FOREVER!

1989 brought many memories. Our family moved from Southern California to Northern California where we bought a house. I turned another year older. We rescued a chicken and had an outhouse in our garage one Christmas when our septic system clogged. Our kitchen also flooded after a winter freeze when our pipes burst. I met a King Snake face-to-face, my son started kindergarten, my youngest started walking, and I was admitted into the hospital. I kept having heart trouble. Looking back, I think any normal person would have been stressed out, but after all the tests were complete my doctor came into my hospital room, stood at the foot of my bed, and said, *"Gina, I'm so sorry to be bringing you such news, but you have heart disease."*

It wasn't until he began to share how sorry he was and wished that he could do more for me when I realized I was in serious trouble. A few hours later my husband came in and said, *"I just spoke with the doctor. I'm so sorry. Is there anything I can do for you?"*

"Please, just go home and be with our children."

In the bed next to me was a woman named Sharon who had just been told that she had lung cancer. Not knowing what to do I grabbed my IV and went and laid next to her in her bed. The two of us talked for hours, both sharing our lives and our feelings about dying, because when one doesn't feel well, dying is not such a scary thing.

As I listened to Sharon talk about her family, I felt so sorry for her. She and her husband, even though they lived together, hadn't spoken in years, and her daughter was not someone she spoke highly about. She didn't sound as if she had the will to live, so when I heard her voice turn into tears, I reached my arms around her and asked, *"Sharon, do you believe in God? Do you believe in Jesus? Do you believe that the only way to enter Heaven is to believe that Jesus is your Lord and Savior and that He died for your sins?"*

"I do," she replied. *"It's the only thing I believe in, and I welcome death."* She continued, *"And, mark my words, when I die my husband and daughter will not have a funeral for me. They will cremate me and leave me at the morgue."*

The more Sharon and I talked, the more I realized that there was a day when I was ready to die. I wanted to die so I could see my father again. And it hit me that I wanted to die for a man who never came looking for me, but now I had children of my own, and I couldn't let them grow up without me.

That evening I couldn't sleep. I kept thinking, what if I die before God calls me to my tree? I can't die. Not yet! So, when Sharon fell asleep and the lights were turned off, I sat up in my bed, reached over to my nightstand and grabbed the little black comb they gave me in the hospital. My hair is very curly and thick, and I just started brushing my hair and praying. I'm writing this moment down, because I still don't remember the night, but I remember one thing.

I prayed.

I asked God this... *"God if You are listening, PLEASE LET ME LIVE. PLEASE ALLOW ME TO LIVE UNTIL MY YOUNGEST CHILD, SHAE, IS 18. IF YOU AL-LOW ME TO LIVE UNTIL SHE IS 18, I PROMISE YOU THAT I WILL DO ANY-THING FOR YOU! I WILL GIVE YOU MY LIFE IN SERVICE AND SERVE YOU THE REST OF MY DAYS!"*

The next morning my husband came in and noticed a large pile of hair lying on the floor, *"Hey. What the heck. Why is there a pile of your hair on the floor?"*

"Oh, God and I were communicating. I believe everything is going to be okay now," I said. I never even noticed the pile of hair; I just knew that my hand was combing my hair and my heart was communicating with God.

It was Thursday, three days after all my hair had fallen to floor, when a doc-tor came into my room and said, *"Gina, we have a doctor who has come from San Francisco to try a medical procedure on you. It may help. Are you willing to allow him to do it?"*

To the ICU I went, and a catheter was inserted into my foot, up my leg, through my groin and up into my heart. As they were doing the procedure I hap-pened to look over to my right and noticed a window with opened curtains and I could see an old woman. As I was looking at her, I felt the most incredible peace come over me, as if her spirit was talking to mine. She was lying silently and was covered up to her neck with a blanket when suddenly, I noticed flashing red lights go off above her bed. A nurse quickly ran in, took her pulse, and then gently cov-ered her face with the blanket. I had just witnessed the death of this woman and for some reason she brought me comfort. I felt as if she wasn't alone and that my heart knew that everything was going to be okay for both of us.

A few moments later my doctor walked over to my side and asked, *"Do you believe in miracles?"*

"Yes!" I half consciously replied.

"Well, Gina. It looks like you've got one and will live another day."

APPOINTMENT ELEVEN CONTINUES...

"So everyone who acknowledges God before men, Jesus also will acknowledge before His Father who is in Heaven, but whoever denies God before men, Jesus also will deny before His Father who is in Heaven." Matthew 10:32-33

It was a Friday, a year from the day that I left the hospital — the year in which my life should have been over, yet I was still alive. I had started a small business with my best friend, Lisa Newman, called Made to Order, that would allow us to sell the crafts of others out of my home. I still wasn't well enough to go into the working world, but I could do something.

So, I ran an advertisement in our local newspaper and asked other crafters to call me if they were interested in our service, and to be honest, I was surprised when my phone actually rang... *"Hello. I'm calling about the ad you ran in the newspaper,"* a voice said.

"Yes. How can I help you?" I replied.

The two of us talked for quite some time and then she asked, *"Gina, do I know you? Your voice and laugh sound very familiar."*

"Well, unless you're a doctor or nurse, I haven't been out in the world for quite a while and..."

Interrupting she asked, *"Hey. Were you hospitalized about a year ago, and were you in the same hospital room with a woman named Sharon?"*

"YES! How is she?"

"She passed away a few months ago on Christmas Eve, and can you believe that her family had her cremated. She never had a funeral, and her ashes are still at the morgue."

For a moment I sat there remembering her words, *"When I die my husband and daughter will not have a funeral for me. They will cremate me and leave me at the morgue."*

"I'm so sorry to hear the news. How long have the two of you been friends?" I asked.

"We were friends for over 20 years and to this day I have one regret."

"One regret?" I asked. *"What is it?"*

"Gina, I believe in God, but Sharon would never talk about her faith. I regret never asking her if she believed that Jesus Christ was her Lord and Savior."

I couldn't believe my ears. *"I have to tell you something,"* I said. *"The day the two of us found out that we had a year to live I crawled in bed with her, and I asked her."*

"And what did she say?"

"She said, 'I do. It's the only thing I believe in, and I welcome death.'"

The woman on the other end of my phone never gave me her name, and we never said goodbye. She just started to cry, and when it became apparent to me that our phone conversation was finished, I very gently hung up the phone.

I now believe that God knew this woman's heart would be hurting over not asking her friend five words, *"DO YOU BELIEVE IN GOD?"* God knew I was searching for the truth. He knew I would ask her. That's why He sent me to the hospital.

My thoughts at this moment: Death is sad, but when we lose someone we love, a parent, child, family member or friend, it makes us think about the afterlife. Where do we go? What happens to us? Seems I never thought about God until I wanted to see my father again or I wanted to live long enough to watch my children grow.

It's interesting that Sharon's friend also thought about death. Even though she believed in God and Jesus, she wasn't brave enough to ask Sharon if she did. Hence, she now was faced with the fear of the unknown for Sharon.

I made a promise to God that I would do anything for Him, and in the simplicity of salvation I think I'll just start out by doing a head count... *"So everyone who acknowledges God before men, Jesus also will acknowledge before His Father* who is in Heaven, but whoever denies God before men, Jesus also will deny before His Father who is in Heaven." Matthew 10:32-33

"[Jesus]I am the way, and the truth, and the life. No one comes to the Father except through Me." John 14:6

"Do you believe Me, Gina?" (Jesus)

"I do!"

Do you?

Appointment Twelve

"YES, GINA. THAT WAS ME."

"Do not neglect to show hospitality to strangers,
for thereby some have entertained angels unawares."
Hebrews 13:2

Reminiscing about one's life is sometimes a hard thing to do. It's difficult to recall all the moments in life that one wants to remember and as I stood in front of my gate, I wasn't sure where the memories of my life were going to take me. The cherubim was waiting, but as I looked at this angelic being, I could only see one of his four faces and within a moment my mind was transported back to one Sunday in the fall.

I was driving up the highway, heading to my sister-in-law's pizza parlor because every Sunday evening, I would come and work for her so she could have one night off.

As I was driving up the highway, I realized that my car was my place of solitude. The place where I would dream, plan what I was going to make for dinner and my secret place where I would talk to God.

The drive that Sunday seemed to last forever. The leaves were changing. Fall had arrived. I remember I was upset that night, and instead of simply talking to God I took my right fist and hitting the top of my headliner I said, *"Okay, God. I must make a decision by tomorrow. I need to have surgery, but they're not sure how my body will react to it. Will You please let me know tonight if this surgery will heal me or kill me?"*

I arrived at the restaurant, put on my happy face, and got to work. A few hours into the evening a man walked in with a woman, and the three of us chatted. When their meal was finished the two of them got up, gave me a hug, thanked me for such wonderful service, and walked out the door. As they happened to be getting in their bright yellow Camaro, I looked out the window and continued watching them as they drove away.

A few hours later I was bending over near the cash register, resting my left hand on the counter, and reaching down with my right hand to collect a pen I had just dropped, when I felt a hand upon my left hand. As I stood up, I noticed it was the man, only he had returned alone.

He then leaned forward and when he arrived near my ear he whispered, *"I have to tell you something. I know that you must make a major decision in your life, and you need to make it soon. I was sent to tell you to go ahead. You'll be fine."*

As he spoke, I couldn't breathe.

He then leaned closer, kissed my cheek and as he leaned backwards, I noticed that he had a BIG gold cross around his neck that stood out as if to say, *"I have heard your request. You'll be okay. I promise."*

I was so overwhelmed that I quickly turned my head away from him so he wouldn't see my eyes fill with tears and when I turned back, he was gone. *"Where did the man go?" I asked the cook behind the counter?"*

"What man?" he asked.

"The man I was just talking to. He came in earlier with a woman and they ordered a garlic pizza and then he just came back a moment ago. Where did he go?"

"Gina, the only people who came in tonight were the family of six. We never made a garlic pizza. Tonight was dead."

"Are you kidding me?" I asked.

"No, Gina. I promise. Are you okay?"

The next morning, I called my doctor and scheduled the surgery. All went well, and the following Sunday, as I was lying in my hospital bed, I looked out the window and I couldn't help but wonder who that man was. Was he an angel? Did God send him to me? No one else remembered him, but now I had to decide what I was going to believe and then once I made my decision, I had to be brave enough to believe it.

Being brave is a hard thing at times, but at that moment I grabbed my notebook and pen, looked up to Heaven and asked, *"God, was that my angel? Was that the angel I will one day meet at my tree? Who was he? Please tell me."*

Within a moment my hand began to scribe...

Today I asked my angel, *"What exactly do you do?"*

I heard a voice say softly, *"I help you to get through."*

Through, I thought to myself. What exactly does that mean?

"The Lord has sent me to you, to help you through your day. The day you spoke to Jesus and asked Him into your heart. The day you received salvation... that's the day I got my start. I'm with you when you're sleeping. I'm with you when you pray. My spirit never leaves you, you're never all alone. I'll be with you until the time comes when God has called you home. And when you arrive in eternity, you will come and see. You'll smile and I'll smile back, and I'll say, 'Yes, Gina, that was me.'"

Appointment Thirteen

"MY INSIGHT'S NAME IS THE HOLY SPIRIT"

"When the Spirit of truth comes, he will guide you into all the truth,
for he will not speak on his own authority, but whatever he hears he will speak,
and he will declare to you the things that are to come."

John 16:13

Two years had passed since my last surgery, and I couldn't believe it when another Wednesday rolled around bringing me back to another hospital visit...

"*You okay, Gina?*" the doctor asked.

"*Yes, I'm fine, but hear me when I say that I will never have another surgery again.*"

"*Okay. We're going to put you under now,*" said the doctor. "*Count backwards from ten. This will be over soon.*"

"*Ten, nine, eight, seven...*"

A few hours later I awoke and found myself lying in the back seat of our car. "*What's going on?*" I asked.

"*Did you tell the doctor that you would never have surgery again?*" my husband asked.

"*I don't know. Maybe. Why?*"

"*The doctor came out from your surgery and said that he wasn't able to do it laparoscopically, and because you said you would never have surgery again, he had to bring you out of the anesthesia."*

"Why didn't you just tell him to do it anyway?" I asked.

"I did, but he said he couldn't because you said you never wanted to have surgery again so now, he has to reschedule. Had you said nothing he could have done it. Next time, don't say a word!"

It was Tuesday of the following week when I found myself in another hospital having yet another surgery. The surgery went well and by the following Monday it was my turn to go home...

"Gina are you ready to go home today?" asked the nurse.

"Yes, but I don't feel right." I replied.

"What do you mean you don't feel right?"

"I don't know, but something isn't right."

A few hours later the doctor came into my room, *"You get to go home today. Are you ready?"*

"Yes," I replied, *"but I don't feel right."*

"What do you mean you don't feel right?" asked the doctor.

Since I couldn't explain how I was feeling they checked me out one more time, told me I was fine, and sent me home.

As I was driving home my husband asked, *"You must be excited to get home."*

"I am, but I don't feel right," I replied.

"You keep saying that Gina, but the doctors say you're fine. When we get home maybe you should just get some rest."

When I arrived home, I went into my room, closed the door, and laid down. I was only in there about an hour when I was overwhelmed with knowing that I had to go to the hospital, so I pulled myself out of bed and walking into the family room I said to my husband, *"Please take me to the hospital now."*

We drove up to the hospital in silence and when we arrived, he left me off at the emergency door, *"I'll park the car and you go in and tell them that you don't feel right. I'll be in soon."*

"What seems to be the problem?" the nurse asked.

"I don't' know, but I don't feel right," I replied.

"Do you hurt anywhere?" she asked.

"No."

"Is it hard to breathe?"

"No."

"Did someone hurt you and you don't want to tell us?"

"NO!"

"Then why are you here?" she asked in aggravation.

I then leaned closer to her and said, *"I don't know, but I don't feel right, and God told me to come to the hospital."*

"Who told you to come to the hospital?" she asked.

"God."

"Well then. Go and sit in the lobby and when we're done seeing all the truly sick people, we will call you in."

We waited for nearly four hours until I heard, *"Gina, please follow me."*

As my husband and I walked into the examining room I heard a voice from behind me ask, *"Gina. I hear that you're not feeling well, but you don't know what's wrong, is that correct?"*

"Yes." I replied.

My husband proceeded to tell them that I had spent the past week in another hospital and that they said I was fine. The doctor then shared that he would call the hospital and get a copy of my blood results that were taken before I left. He walked out and another hour went by. We sat until the doctor came in, *"Well, Gina, we're still waiting to hear back from the other hospital. How do you feel now?"*

"I don't feel..."

But right as I began to finish my sentence my arms started floating beside my body and I started to have a seizure. At that moment a nurse flung open the door and said, *"The hospital just called. Her body is completely depleted of potassium and she's in danger of going into cardiac arrest."*

I don't remember anything after that. I passed out. When I awoke, I looked to my right and a bag of potassium was entering my body and my doctor was sitting beside me, *"Well Gina. I don't know what to say to you. I don't know what gave you enough insight to come to the hospital, but had you not been here, you might not be here now. I'm sorry we didn't rush you in sooner."*

A few hours later, as I was walking out of the hospital, I stopped the doctor and said, *"When you were sitting beside me in the room you said that you didn't know what gave me enough insight to come to the hospital and I wanted to let you know that my insight's name is the Holy Spirit."*

Appointment Fourteen

"WRITTEN FOR THE LORD'S BLESSINGS"

"And all these blessings shall come upon you and overtake you,
if you obey the voice of the Lord *your God."*

Deuteronomy 28:2

It was just another Wednesday at work when the phone rang, so I reached for the receiver and before I could place it next to my ear, I heard the panicked voice ask, *"Gina, are you there? Can you hear me?"*

"Yes, I hear you."

"I don't know how to tell you this, but Lloyd passed away today." I was given the details of his death, and while the panicked voice was speaking it seemed that my memory began to wander back to the year before...

...It was Saturday when my friend, Pat Wirtz, knocked on my front door, *"Gina, I'm heading to an equine open house, and I want you to come with me. Get your coat. Let's go!"* I looked over at my husband, he nodded with a smile and out the door I went.

Bryant Arabians was situated off of Colfax Highway, in the beautiful foothills of the Sierra Nevadas, and could only be entered if the gate was open or if one had the gate code. That Saturday the gate was open and the two of us drove through with excitement. I had never seen such a beautiful ranch and I couldn't wait to park our car. I wanted to see what awaited me beyond the barn. As I got out of the car, that is when I saw her. Darla Bryant was Lloyd's wife, and she was gathering all of us to take us on a tour. I remember she was wearing a white pantsuit and she didn't have a single hair out of place. She spoke for a moment and then the crowd followed her out into her pastures. Each pasture was filled with the most beautiful Arabian horses I had ever seen, and as the crowd seemed to follow the hoof prints of the horses, I found myself following Darla.

"Excuse me," I said. *"You have the most beautiful ranch I have ever seen. I sure wish that I could afford one of your horses."*

She smiled and the two of us walked around her ranch for over an hour talking about their horses. A month later Darla called and told me that she had a little filly whose owner wanted to sell her, *"I guess they're not going to be able to keep her, so she wants to find a good home and is only charging what it cost for the stud fee to our stallion, El Hadiyyah."*

That evening my family and I had a meeting and the next day we purchased, Anshulla, which defined means: God willing. And it was. It was God's will that took us on the rest of our journey together.

Here begins what I want to remember…

…A week after we had purchased Anshulla, Lloyd called and asked me if I would like to bring her back to show her off at another open house they were having. I immediately said, *"YES!"* My family and I arrived, and we paraded her around, and when it was time for us to load her up, I walked over to Lloyd and said, *"If you ever need anyone to help in your office, I'm your gal."*

He laughed and replied, *"Gina, you have no idea how many people have offered to work for us."*

"No, I don't. That doesn't matter to me." I replied. *"I just know that I would be a good employee."*

The following Monday my phone rang. *"Hello,"* I said.

"Hello. Is Gina there?"

"Yes, sir. How many I help you?" I replied.

"Okay, smarty pants. Darla and I were talking, and if you think you can work for us then I'll give you a try."

I worked three days a week for a year, and during that time Darla and I became the best of friends. My fondest memory of Lloyd was — one day I came to work and was having a bad morning. Instead of doing work, Darla turned her chair towards me and simply listened. We saw Lloyd walk by the office window a few times, but he said nothing. As I was leaving for the day, Lloyd met me at my car, *"I noticed you and Darla talked all morning. Do you feel better?"* he asked.

"Yes, thank you." I replied.

"Well, good. And just so you know, I'm not paying you for today. I'm not here to pay for your therapy."

We laughed and off I went.

Lloyd and Darla had been married for ten years and to celebrate their anniversary they went to Hawaii... As I sat in the office, I realized I was still holding the receiver up to my ear. I couldn't believe that I had just received a phone call sharing that Lloyd had passed away. He was fine three days ago. He looked great, and now the panicked voice on the phone was telling me that he had passed away.

Tests concluded that Lloyd had cancer unaware and by the time he found out it was too late. It was Saturday when they laid Lloyd's body to rest. Hundreds of people showed up for his Celebration of Life, and it was there where Darla asked me to come and work with her full time. I accepted.

As time moved on, so did everyone else. It seemed rather quickly all the cards, calls and visits stopped and two weeks later it was just she and I. It was Monday when I came into work and found her crying at her desk, *"What's wrong?"* I asked. *"Are you okay?" "I just got a phone call that my son, Jeff, was hit by a car and lost his right arm. I need to go to him."*

Darla wiped the tears from her face and that was the moment I was first introduced to faith. I couldn't help but wonder how God would allow one woman to go through so much in such a short amount of time, yet I never once heard her be angry or blame God for anything. She seemed to have  this inner love for God and a strength that I couldn't explain. All I could do was watch.

It was Thursday (six months later) when I had come to work and without saying hello, I said, *"DARLA, you're not going to believe this, but last night I had a dream about Lloyd."* I then grabbed my chair, sat down, and positioned myself so I could look directly into her eyes.

"It was so real. I was walking up to a house that was situated in the woods. It was a two-story house, sort of faded by the sun. There were two steps that led up to the front porch and when I arrived at the door, I knocked. Situated to the left of the door I could see a faded light through the window, but nothing else. When the door opened it was Lloyd. He didn't say anything to me but motioned for me to walk through the door. I came in, he closed the door behind me, and then he began to walk up a flight of stairs that was immediately positioned to our right. When we arrived at the top of the stairs, I noticed to the left there was only one door, and the door was closed. Lloyd opened the door, and I followed him inside. When we both were in the room, there was no window — only a wooden chair situated under a writing desk, a white piece of paper and a red pen. Lloyd then picked up the red pen and handing it to me he said, 'When you write, and you will, sign everything, L.B.'

'What?' I asked him.

'When you write, and you will, sign everything, L.B.' Then I woke up. What do you think that means?" I asked Darla.

We talked for a while about the dream and then decided that from that day onward we would sign all her letters with an L.B., and that maybe it was Lloyd's way of making sure he wasn't forgotten... after all, those were his initials. In all actuality we had no idea what it meant, but my heart felt that I needed to trust it.

After our discussion and the passing of months, I continued to write L.B. on everything and with time I noticed that every time I sat down with a pen or at my computer words would flow as if I was being dictated to. I couldn't understand it, but for some reason I couldn't stop writing. Then one Sunday afternoon my husband and I were in our barn, raking, when I said to him, *"I still have no idea why my heart needs to write L.B. on everything?"* And within the simplicity of breathing, my husband stopped raking and said, *"The words that you write are blessings from the Lord, so every time you write you're receiving the Lord's blessings."*

Evening came, and as I was getting into bed, I asked God, *"Is it true? Am I receiving Your blessings?"*

When morning arrived, I found myself holding a piece of paper in my right hand and noticed a pen lying on the floor next to me. Not knowing what to expect I turned the paper over, and this is what I read:

I wake up for gifts so I can share them with others, who am I to kid?

What gifts do I have that another would want?

Not a talent. Not me!

I write things down when I hear Your words,

They speak silently, like a dim light.

They soothe me and protect me —

They guide me through the night.

Not a talent I have that I could share,

I write some words on a pad by my bed,

And then in the morning I read what You said.

Not a talent I have that I could explain —

God calls. I listen. I write what I hear,

And no longer will I question that God isn't near!

I guess that it's good, not a talent I have,

I'm never too busy to hear what God said!

L.B.

It was Monday, the following evening, and not trusting what I had written the night before I asked, *"God. Why are you really waking me up?"*

I fell asleep and the next morning, next to my pen, was a tiny piece of paper that read:

The back of the paper represents the real story. The story not shared with others, but what truly lies within your heart. No one will ever know the real you unless you turn the paper over and finish the story. There's a story for you and one for ME, and one for the rest of the world to read. Keep writing!

L.B.

Appointment Fifteen

"YOU'RE THE LUCKY ONE"

"Beloved, if God so loved us,
we also ought to love one another."
1 John 4:11

It was Monday and I found myself again, lying in a bed in the hospital; only this time was different. I was different. Somehow my heart knew I was there because God had made an appointment for me to be there. I knew that my life was no longer about my wants or needs, because I promised God that if He allowed me to live until Shae was 18, I would do anything for Him. I was starting to understand that with each year that I lived, God had honored my request, and with each hospital visit He was seeing if I was still willing to keep my promise, and simply pay attention.

"Okay, God. I'm here." I said. *"You made this appointment now please tell me the rest of Your story."*

A few moments later I saw an elderly man walk past my room. He was wearing a torn shirt, pants that were too large, shoes that were riddled with holes and he was holding a single, white rose. He looked directly at me, and then continued onward. The next day I saw him walk past my room again. He looked in and was gone, and I couldn't help but wonder whom he was looking for.

Three days had passed since he had walked past my hospital room, and while I was in the bathroom changing to be discharged, I was feeling disappointed.

I knew that God had sent me there for a reason, yet I was leaving with nothing. Yes, I was getting the medical help that I needed, but I felt like I missed His message and was feeling a bit defeated until...

I walked out of the bathroom and there it was. The rose. As I began to walk towards it, I heard my nurse's voice from behind my medical file, say, *"Oh, you're the lucky one today."*

"Excuse me?"

"You're the lucky one today. He gave you the white rose."

"What do you mean?" I asked.

"It's a sad, but rather beautiful story," she said. *"A few years ago, his wife was diagnosed with cancer. She loved white roses, so every day after work he would stop and get her a single, white rose. One night he was working late and couldn't pick one up, but when he arrived home, he saw the disappointment on her face. So, he left and drove all over town until he was able to find her, her single, white rose. When he returned home, he found her peaceful. She had passed away while he was gone. Two weeks after her death he began showing up at the hospital, with her single, white rose. He only gives his roses out to the person that he believes will understand his message. Read the note."*

As I picked up the rose, I noticed there was a piece of paper that was attached which read: *We never know when our last hour will arrive. Learn to enjoy the little things in life. For they are the big things, because like this rose... this rose will lose its fragrance and the petals will dry and fall to the floor. This rose will soon be no more. BUT... the memory of its fragrance and the beauty of this rose will remain within you forever. We can only understand a gift of love when it's unexpected, because love is the only gift that we can give to another and give it freely. Always remember I love you and I expect nothing from you in return.*

When I got home, I went and placed my rose on the nightstand next to my bed, and I kept thinking about how I thought he was looking for someone he couldn't find. I thought he may have been homeless. I thought so many things that were not his truths, but what I learned from this appointment was that through the loss of his wife, he kept her memory alive by delivering love into the rooms of people who were scared and alone, or people like me... I was looking for God's message.

The greatest thing I learned from his giving was when I am hurting the most is when I need to give a gift away in love, so my heart won't become bitter with sadness. Maybe that's why God gave His Son out of love. Had He done it with anger, He too might have become bitter to the people He was trying to save. Like Connie's father who would always remind his wife what love is... God too shares that love is patient, love is kind. It does not envy, it does not boast, it is not proud. It does not dishonor others, it is not self-seeking, it is not easily angered, it keeps no record of wrongs. Love does not delight in evil but rejoices with truth. It always protects, always trusts, always hopes, always perseveres. Love never fails. (1 Corinthians 13:4-8)

Written for *The Lord's Blessings*

Appointment Sixteen

"MOM, I'M READY"

"That which is born of the flesh is flesh,
and that which is born of the Spirit is spirit."
John 3:6

It was Sunday when I had been standing outside my son's Sunday school class when he walked outside of the room and said, *"Mom, I'm ready."*

"Ready for what, Glenn?"

"I'm ready to be baptized!"

"Well then. You need to walk over and talk to Pastor Morton and tell him."

Glenn noticed Pastor Morton across the church and smiling back at me, he ran off and I followed closely behind. Pastor Morton happened to be talking with someone and noticed that Glenn was patiently waiting for him to finish his conversation, *"Hello Glenn. What can I do for you today?"* he asked.

"I'm ready to be baptized!"

"You are?"

"Yes, I am."

"Okay. This week I will come over to your house and the two of us will sit down at your kitchen table and we'll talk about it. Does that work for you?"

"Yes, sir. See you soon."

The following Thursday Pastor Morton showed up at our home, *"Hello, Gina.*

Is Glenn here? I'm here to visit with him."

"GLENN, PASTOR MORTON IS HERE FOR YOU!" I yelled with excitement.

The two of them went and sat at our kitchen table. I left the room, but I only went as far as to where they couldn't see me, but I could hear them... *"Glenn, you believe you want to be baptized. Do you know what that means?"* Pastor Morton asked.

"Yes, I do. It means that I believe that Jesus Christ is the one true Son of God, He died for my sins, and I believe the only way to enter Heaven is to know that God is real."

The two of them talked for nearly an hour and then Pastor Morton got up from the table, walked over to my son, and extending his right hand towards his he said, *"Glenn, it will be an honor to baptize you into the family of God. I'll see you on Sunday."*

On Sunday, the 3rd day of March, my 12-year-old son stepped into a warm pool of water and gave his whole heart to the Lord. As I sat there and watched I began to think back to when I was 12, and for a moment I was holding a piece of broken glass and a pack of unopened cigarettes wondering how I would end my life. It was then when I realized the difference between my son and me. When I was 12, I couldn't see beyond 12, but my son could now see the kingdom of God... and Jesus answered him, *"Truly, truly, I say to you, unless one is born again he cannot see the kingdom of God."* John 3:3

Two weeks later the mail arrived with my son's Spiritual Rebirth Certificate, and I must admit that his baptism certificate means more to me than his actual birth certificate, because Glenn had no choice to be born into this world, but it was his choice to be born into the 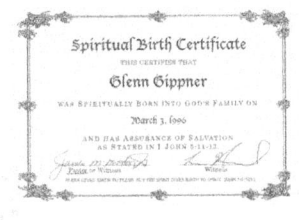 next. And my husband and I don't always agree, but I never want to forget how grateful I am that he did not allow me to baptize our son as an infant, because this moment might have never happened. My prayer from this day onward is that Glenn never forgets what he did, why he did it, and whom he did it for.

Written for *The Lord's Blessings*

Appointment Seventeen

"PRAYING PLAY-BY-PLAY"

"Therefore encourage one another and
build one another up, just as you are doing."
1 Thessalonians 5:11

It was Tuesday morning when my son asked, *"Mom. Are you going to come to my basketball game after school?"*

"Glenn, I would love to come," I replied *"but you rarely get to play, and I have a ton of stuff that I need to get done this afternoon, so no. Probably not."*

Where that came from, I had no idea, and I immediately tried to backtrack what I had said, but it was too late. So, I stopped talking and waited for him to speak.

"Mom, the game isn't about me. It's about the team. The best players, play."

"You're right. I'll be there!"

That afternoon I arrived early and found myself a quiet place on the bleachers where I wouldn't be tempted to talk to my dear friend, Angie Montre. Angie and I met one day when we pulled into the school parking lot. We had both jumped out of our trucks, and when we saw each other, we smiled. It seemed that the two of us both drove trucks, and our trucks were both filled with hay. Both of us had long, curly hair, and we were both wearing overalls. The minute we saw each other I said, *"Hey, what are the chances of this?"* We looked like twins, and from that moment on we were friends. Our boys were also friends and played on the same basketball team, so we would sit by each other and talk. When my son was on the court we'd stop talking and we'd watch. When her son, Kyle, was on the court we'd stop talking and we'd watch. The problem was neither one of them was on the court much, so we talked a lot, and it wasn't until I stopped talking that I was able to truly see my son.

This is what I saw...

...I saw my son sitting next to his friends on the bench, enjoying the fact that he was part of the team and not a bystander in the bleachers.

...I saw my son's face when someone got hurt.

...I saw my son pray when someone went to make an impossible shot.

...I saw the confidence my son had in himself because he didn't need to be the star of the team, but a friend to the players.

When the game was over, and the two of us arrived home, I couldn't stop thinking about what I had learned from watching my son, and because I never wanted to forget the moment, I grabbed a piece of paper and began to write...

Sitting on the sidelines is the toughest job to have,

Knowing everything to do,

Just not given the chance.

But then you have a moment when you're out there on the court,

You pass the ball to someone; they shoot the ball and score!

Back on the bench again the quarter has just ended,

Now, the game is getting close, the crowds are getting louder.

They shoot the ball and miss; time is getting shorter.

The players are too busy to bow their heads and pray,

When God reminds you why you're not supposed to play.

"You did not make the team for anyone but Me! I needed some that

understood the real rules of the game, and that's why I chose you to

sit upon this bench. So, when you're on the sideline your position is in play...

Look to Me for guidance.

Bow your head and pray!

For I like to see you cheering,
I like the team that wins,
I like the team that loses to try all over again!
But my favorite part of the game is not the game per se,
My greatest joy comes from the bench, praying to Me, play-by-play."
Written for *The Lord's Blessings*

Appointment Eighteen

"GOD DRIVES OUR CAR"

"The LORD will keep your going out and your coming in
from this time forth and forevermore."
Psalm 121:8

I've travelled many roads within my life. Some were beautiful, so serene that I would use any excuse to take them. Some roads led me to the coast, where the sea breeze would remind me of my childhood. Some roads put me in the middle of traffic where I couldn't wait to get off, and some roads took me to the desert, where the heat would have been unbearable had I not been in the comforts of my air-conditioned car.

Yes, there are so many roads in my life that I have driven on, but there was one road that always required a decision. Turn right and go the winding, scenic route or turn left and go straight. No turns. No views. Nothing more than a drive. I always turned right.

It was Wednesday and I had errands to run so I asked my daughter, Shae, if she wanted to go with me and she agreed. As we were driving, we got to the fork in the road where we needed to make one decision, *"Shae, do you want to go right or left?"* I asked.

"I don't care."

"Are you sure?" I asked. This road always made her feel uneasy, but because she allowed me to make the decision I turned right, and silence fell over our car.

We drove for at least five minutes before I heard, *"Mom, God drives our car just like I drive my Hot Wheels."*

"What?" I asked.

"God drives our car just like I drive my Hot Wheels. When I'm playing with my Hot Wheels I can decide if I want to crash into something or I can decide if I want my car to get there safely. I'm in control of my car. God does what I do, and He guides the cars on the road. He will make sure that we get up this winding road, safely. Right?"

Within a moment I finally understood why she never wanted to turn right. The road had many turns, and she couldn't see beyond the bends. She concluded by saying, *"Mom, if we don't get to where we're going safely it was because God has another plan for our lives or He's tired of us driving our old car and will provide us with a new one, right?"*

As I looked over at her I could see the face of a child who had prayed for peace from worrying about what she could not see, and God had given her an answer that she could understand. There was no need for me to answer her. The peace that arrived within her face told me that she didn't need my approval for what she believed.

The next morning, I had gone to work at Darla's, and as she was going through her mail she stopped, turned to me and asked, *"Hey, do you want this?"*

I reached for the envelope and when I looked inside there was a picture of Jesus and He was standing over a freeway holding His hand above the cars. The moment I saw it tears came to my eyes and I knew what I was going to do with it.

So, that evening, after dinner, I invited Shae to take a walk with me and the two of us walked down to my car, and I opened the passenger door, and invited her to sit down. She smiled, jumped in the seat and I shut the door. I then walked over to the driver's side and climbed in, *"Here, I have a gift for you. It arrived in the mail today."*

I can still see her face as she peeked into the envelope and without pulling it out her eyes showed me that God had confirmed her heart.

"Go ahead. Take it out of the envelope," I said.

Then handing her some tape I said, *"Here. Put this tape on the back of the picture and we'll place Jesus right here on the dash of our car where we both can remember that God drives our car just like you drive your Hot Wheels, and one day, Shae... when it's your turn to drive, we'll take this picture and place it in your car so you'll never forget that Jesus always calls, 'shotgun.'"*

Written for *The Lord's Blessings*

Appointment Nineteen

"HAVE YOU EVER SEEN A TEACUP?"

"In the same way also He took the cup, after supper, saying,
'This cup is the new covenant in My blood.
Do this, as often as you drink it, in remembrance of Me.'"
1 Corinthians 11:25

It was Saturday when I realized how many things I had collected through the years. My children always seemed to accuse me of not being able to throw anything away and looking around I'm discovering that everything I own once belonged to someone that I love.

Possessions that others worked hard to obtain and then at a point in their lives when they no longer wanted or needed it, they'd give it to me. I have a hard time letting go of a memory.

To me, a possession without a memory is like a child without a mother. Where did it come from?

My finest possessions came from my grandmother. She worked hard for what she had and was proud of what she owned. I have a teacup collection that every time I walk by it, I'm reminded of the moment she gave them to me.

It was Sunday and I was 17 years old. I had gone to visit my grandparents and was standing outside when I heard my grandmother's voice yell, *"GINA. COME INTO THE KITCHEN. I WANT TO ASK YOU SOMETHING."*

"Yes. What is it?"

"I want you to look around my house and pick out something you like, because when I die, I want you to have something from me. Now, go on. Pick something."

"I don't want anything. Why are you talking like this?" I asked. *"I want you to live forever and..."*

But before I could finish my sentence, she interrupted me.

"Stop being silly. No one lives forever. Now, pick something. Do it now before I get mad, and you ruin this moment."

Without thinking I pointed to her antique teacup collection that was her mother's and without saying a word she walked out of the room and returned with a box and some old newspaper, *"Well, don't just stand there,"* she said, *"help me pack up your teacups."*

Neither one of us said a word. We just packed the teacups, and when we were done, she placed the box by her front door and said, *"When you leave today do not forget to take your cups. They are for you to remember me by."*

Decades had passed and my grandmother had come for one of her visits. It was a Saturday when she happened to notice her cups on my wall and almost as if she was seeing them for the first time she said, *"Gina, I just wanted to give you something that would remind you of me."*

"I'm so glad you gave them to me," I said. *"I'm happy I picked the cups, because they were something I could hold on to."*

The two of us got a little emotional and then at the exact same time we said, *"You know I have a favorite cup!"* Then smiling at each other we both reached up and our hands touched as we both reached for the same one. Out of the ten teacups that sat on the shelf, we both liked the black one with the pink roses. Then, later that same evening, as I was getting ready for bed, I reached for my Bible. I had to find something...

"And he said, 'Jesus, remember me when You come into Your kingdom.' And He said to him, 'Truly, I say to you, today you will be with Me in paradise.'" Luke 23:42-43

Just as my grandmother wanted me to remember her, a thief on the cross wanted to be remembered by Jesus. I believe that at the end of our life, it doesn't matter who we are within our life, we want to know that we will be remembered by someone.

As I got into bed that evening, I grabbed a piece of paper and pen and left it on my nightstand. I then looked up to Heaven and said, *"Please give me words that I can give to my grandmother so she will know that I will never forget her. Wake me so I can write. AMEN!"*

The next morning, I looked on my nightstand and there were words which read:

Have you ever seen a teacup, the way it draws you near?
A cup of tea immediately takes away even the darkest of fears.
Have you ever seen a teacup as it shimmers in the light?
It smiles at you softly, whispering, everything will be alright.
Have you ever seen a teacup when there are two to share?
The stories and the laughter not a soul would dare...
To ever interrupt what's being shared between those cups.
Have you ever seen a teacup early in the morn?
Or right before the rain or when a baby is born?
Have you ever seen a teacup before you went to bed?
You think of all the things you did and all the things you said.
Have you ever seen a teacup when a mother sits?
Just long enough to listen, how the two seem to fit.
Have you ever seen a teacup when you don't know what to do?
A teacup, like a grandmother, can make all your dreams come true.
Written for *The Lord's Blessings* in memory of my grandmother, Kay Misken

Appointment Twenty

"MY DEAREST PAT"

"Every good gift and every perfect gift is from above, coming down from
the Father of lights with whom there is no variation or shadow due to change."
James 1:7

It was Wednesday and I had to run to the store, but prior to this day I had heard that my dear friend, Pat Wirtz, was diagnosed with cancer, and when I arrived at the store, I turned to walk down the milk aisle and there she was...

"Hey, Pat. How are you doing?" I asked.

I didn't want to say anything about her cancer unless she did. I knew all too well that some moments in life are personal and if she wanted to share the news, I would receive it. If not, it would go unspoken.

"Gina, I was diagnosed with lung cancer, and I'm just doing my best to get through it."

"I'm so sorry," I said.

"My only prayer is that if God decides that He wants to take me home, I don't want to die in pain."

The two of us continued to talk about life, we reminisced about the day we went to Darla's, and what a wonderful day that was and how we were looking for-ward to the fall and then I said, *"Pat, if you need anything at all, please call me."*

We hugged and both went our own way.

As I was driving home, I noticed a tree that looked like the tree that God had given me to plant in His garden, and I immediately began to think about my tree. Was it still alive? Had it grown? If today were the day that God called me to my tree, what would I do? It seemed that at that moment, the reality of Pat, and her one request, brought me back to my tree and for the first time I wondered... Was Pat given a tree? Was everyone given a tree? So, I decided I would pull my car over and walk to the tree. Standing within a respectful distance, I said, *"God, if You could please show me something that I could give to Pat to bring her comfort during this time in her life I would greatly appreciate it. Thank You and Amen!"*

I got back in my car and as I was driving, I saw a vision of a quilt that had fifteen quilt squares with seven scripture verses. I smiled and said out loud, *"Oh, You want me to make her a comfort quilt!"*

As soon as I returned home, I went directly to my closet and found the fabric I was going to use. I then cut out seven squares of white fabric, and eight squares of a beautiful, floral print. I found seven scripture verses which represented comfort and carefully wrote them on the fabric with permanent ink and then I sewed them together. By 5:30pm Pat's Comfort Quilt was complete. The next morning a friend stopped by, noticed the quilt, and asked if she could have it for a friend who needed comfort. I couldn't seem to say no, so I gave it to her. I then got out more fabric and made another quilt and within two days that quilt was needed for another.

For the next few months, it seemed that each time I would make a quilt, God would instruct my heart to give it away. Then another Friday rolled around, and I was downtown at our local Farmer's Market when my daughter, Heidi, came running up to me and said, *"Mom. Did you hear? Pat had a stroke and she's in the hospital."*

My heart skipped a beat, and I immediately left the market. When I arrived home, I put on a pot of coffee, cut out the last of my fabric and then as I reached for my Bible I looked up to Heaven and said, *"God, I'm so sorry I didn't get Pat her quilt. I don't even know what verses to use. Please help me. I'm going to close my eyes; open the Bible and I need You to please point my finger to the seven scriptures YOU want me to place on her quilt. AMEN!"*

By the following morning, I had completed her quilt, put on another pot of coffee, jumped in the shower and by 9:00am I arrived at the hospital with my coffee in tote.

As I was getting out of my car I noticed Pat's husband, Roy, and their grandson, Luke. I motioned for them to come over so I could give them the quilt. When Luke saw it, he grabbed it from my hands and asked if he could give it to her, *"Of course,"* I said. *"It's my gift for you to give."*

As I was turning to leave Roy asked, *"Where are you going, Gina? Please come with us. She loves you and would love to hear your voice."*

The three of us walked silently up to her room and when we arrived Pat was lying on her bed, lifeless. The stroke had left her unable to speak. She had no use of her left side, and she didn't seem to move at all.

"Pat," Roy said, *"Gina made you this beautiful quilt that Luke is holding and we're going to cover you with it. I will read to you what it says."*

Roy began reading the scriptures, when suddenly, she slowly began moving her right arm and with what little strength she had she reached for the quilt and pulled it up to her chin, and that was the last time Pat ever moved.

As I was leaving, Roy asked if I would come back that evening and stay the night with her. He too wasn't well and needed some rest. I agreed and at 9:00pm I arrived back at the hospital.

"Thank you, Gina for doing this. There's nothing they can do for her now. All we can do is pray and wait. The cancer has taken over her body and the stroke has left her completely paralyzed on her left side. All we can do is see what the Good Lord decides, but it brings me comfort to know that she's no longer in pain. Oh, and if you'd like there's a notebook on the shelf that her friends have been writing in. My prayer is that God will heal her body and when she's feeling better, she can read the prayers and well wishes from her friends."

As Roy was walking out the door, he turned off the lights, and opening her hospital room door he said, *"I'll leave this door cracked so you have just enough light, so you are not left in the dark."*

I sat in the chair next to her and silence immediately fell over the room. As my eyes focused through the darkness, I happened to notice the notebook, so I walked over and picked it up. I wasn't going to write anything because I wasn't sure what to write. So, I started reading and within minutes my eyes were filled with tears. Everyone commented that when they came to see her, they were not sure what to write, but assured her that while she was sleeping, they each read her the scriptures that were written on her quilt.

I sat next to Pat all night. I didn't want to fall asleep because I knew those hours were precious. I knew I would never see her again. I knew because of her prayer not to die in pain... *"My only prayer is that if God decides He wants to take me home. I don't want to die in pain."* She was no longer in pain.

As I sat with her, I decided I would write something within the notebook and when I was finished, I tore it out and placed it within my wallet.

On Sunday, Roy arrived at the hospital at 9:00am. I stayed with him until 11:55am, and five minutes later, at 12:00 noon, Pat went to be with the Lord.

The following Saturday my children and I went to Pat's Celebration of Life, and I immediately placed us in the back of the church because I felt that I had been given a gift of time with her that was precious. For some reason God allowed me to spend the last night of her life with her, and even though we sat in silence, it was greatest gift I could have ever been given. The gift of time.

As Pat's Celebration of Life was ending, I looked over and noticed that Roy had been clutching the comfort quilt through the whole service, and it was then when the pastor looked over at Roy and said, *"Before we head to the reception, I want to share one more story. It's a love story about a man, his wife, and a quilt...*

Pat and Roy were married for over 40 years and each night, right before they would go to sleep, Roy would walk over to Pat's side of the bed, and he would tuck her in. Pat had a habit of falling out of bed, and because Roy loved her so, he wanted her to feel secure. A week ago, today, Roy took one more walk around her bedside, only instead of tucking her in with a blanket, he tucked her in with the quilt that he's holding. The quilt has scriptures written on it, so he covered her with God's words and within a moment, Pat went to be with the Lord. She was comforted."

It's funny how one moment in time can change everything. Here I had felt so guilty because I had given so many quilts away and didn't get one to Pat until I thought it was too late, but what God was showing me was... by the pastor sharing that story... was had I made it for her sooner the quilt would have been at home and would not have been with her at the hospital. I had no idea that Roy tucked her in each night, but God did.

After her Celebration of Life was over, I dropped my children off at home and drove back to the tree where I had first prayed for Pat. I knelt and placed an envelope against the tree. Inside the envelope was the letter that I wrote to Pat on the last evening of her life.

The letter read...

My dearest Pat,

Have you even noticed that some quilts are inspired from above? They bring us warmth and comfort, and some have imprints of My love. A quilt can be many things, but when they're touched by My hand... The moment you feel its fabric, that's the moment you understand. Soon you will be with Me in Heaven, and your pain will be no more. I will be waiting for you standing at Heaven's door. Sleep well, my dearest Pat. I'll see you soon, and love will be by your side. Your name has been written in My book, and it includes the story of your life!

Written for *The Lord's Blessings*

Patricia Wirtz was 64 when she passed away and is buried at the Penn Valley Cemetery in Penn Valley, CA. She was loved by many. I was one of them.

Appointment Twenty-One

"10, 2, 1902"

"Are we beginning to commend ourselves again? Or do we need, as some do, letters of recommendation to you, or from you? You yourselves are our letter of recommendation, written on our hearts, to be known and read by all. And you show that you are a letter from Christ delivered by us, written not with ink but with the Spirit of the living God, not on tablets of stone but on tablets of human hearts."

2 Corinthians 3:1-3

It was Thursday and I was out cleaning my garage when I came upon a box that had tons of old envelopes that were dated from another time, so the writer in me had to stop what I was doing and investigate, but when I found nothing, except empty envelopes, I decided to put all the envelopes back into the box and throw them away. As I was walking to the trash I tripped and the box flew out of my hand, and as I was getting up, I noticed a single letter falling from the sky.

I was intrigued so I opened the envelope and was surprised when I found a letter. The letter was dated 10, 2, 1902 — the writing was calligraphy, penned in ink and was written from a son to his mother, explaining how he was adjusting to college life and was missing the smell of her hot breakfast rolls and her hugs of comfort. His life seemed fresh and exciting and not as fast as the world is today.

As I held the letter of a son's heart, I couldn't help but think of all the ribbons tied around cards and letters received from men and women who were off fighting wars. I thought about once upon a time when letters were the only way of communicating with someone who lived in another town or a far-off land. As time progressed the world moved on to the telegraph, telephone, beepers, fax machines, e-mails, cell phones, etc. The only thing we seem to be missing these days is the personal touch.

After I was done reading the letter, I picked up all the fallen envelopes, threw the box away, and placed the letter back in its envelope. I then took the envelope and placed it in another envelope and addressed it to the address it was originally addressed to. Then for the grand finale I grabbed a piece of paper and wrote:

To Whoever Lives Here,

Once upon a time this young man lived within your home. I wasn't sure what to do with the letter, so I decided I would send it back to the house in which it was sent to. I thought it might interest you to know that your house once smelled of hot, breakfast rolls that made a son long for the comforts of home.

Sincerely,

The woman who loves letters from the past

Then later that evening, as I was washing dishes, I couldn't stop thinking about letters and how intimate a letter can be. So, at that moment I dried my last dish, placed my towel on the dish rack and went and found my Bible, opening it to 2 Corinthians 1 and read...

"Paul, an apostle of Christ Jesus by the will of God and Timothy our brother. To the church of God in Corinth, together with all His holy people throughout Achaia; Grace and peace to you from God our Father and the Lord Jesus Christ." Then he continues... *"Praise be to the God and Father of our Lord Jesus Christ, the Father of compassion, and the God of all comfort, who comforts us in all our troubles, so that we can comfort those in any trouble with the comfort we ourselves receive from God. For just as we share abundantly in the sufferings of Christ, so also our comfort abounds through Christ. If we are distressed, it is for your comfort and salvation; if we are comforted, it is for your comfort, which produces in your patient endurance of the*

same sufferings we suffer. And our hope for you is firm because we know that just as you share in our sufferings, so also you share in our comfort."

I continued reading until I realized that people don't change. Thoughts don't change. The need for comfort doesn't change. The only thing that changes is the way we communicate and that's when I decided I would write a letter and place it within my Bible for my children to one day find and that's what I did.

The letter reads:

Dear Glenn, Heidi and Shae,

Gina, a scribe of Christ Jesus by the will of God, I want to share with each of you how I read a book about a man who will never leave your side; He speaks to you and listens; He holds His head with pride. A man born to die because we sinned; He takes our cares away. He hears your every thought; He hears you when you pray. He listens so intently you can hear Him through your heart: Everyday a new beginning; everyday a brand-new start. He left you a simple book because He cared enough to say... "Heaven and Earth will pass away, but My words shall not." Matthew 24:35

Written for The Lord's Blessings

A few months later I received a letter addressed to me and it read:

To the woman who loves letters from the past.

I want you to know that once again, the house smells of hot breakfast rolls and my grandfather was right. The aroma brings comfort.

Sincerely,

The granddaughter who loves the smell of hot, breakfast rolls

APPOINTMENT TWENTY-TWO

"A MOMENT TO REMEMBER"

"O LORD, You hear the desire of the afflicted;
You will strengthen their heart; You will incline Your ear."
Psalm 10:17

It was Monday and I had to take Darla to the hospital. She had an appointment for her pre-op and while she was getting her lab work done, I found a quiet place in the waiting room.

As I was getting myself situated, I happened to look across the room and noticed an elderly woman. She reminded me so much of my husband's grandmother, Rosie, that I couldn't help but stare at her, *"Mom."* Her daughter said loudly. *"The doctors can't seem to find anything wrong with you and..."*

At that moment a nurse interrupted her and said, *"We're going to borrow your mom for a moment. She's in good hands,"* and off the two went.

Nearly 20 minutes went by when I noticed the daughter was crying so I got up from my chair, found her a Kleenex, and handing it to her I asked, *"Are you okay?"*

"What do you do for a woman who still sets the table for two?" she asked.

I smiled and said, *"Love her."*

From the age of the daughter, I had to assume that her mother had to be well into her 80s.

"Don't you think it's odd for a woman who lost her husband (my father) three months ago to continue setting the table for two?" She continued through her tears... *"You see, my husband left me and I'm now going through a divorce, and you don't see me setting my table for two. AND, on top of everything else, she thinks she's sick. They can't find anything wrong with her, and I'm the one she should be worried about. Her husband left her because he died. My husband left me because he didn't want me anymore."*

After a few minutes the words the daughter was saying became a blur. There was no compassion within her voice. The conversation had become all about her and her feelings and as I was caught up in my own thoughts I heard, *"HEY LADY... AREN'T YOU LISTENING TO ME?"* She yelled.

"I know what's wrong with her," I said. *"Her heart is broken, and because your heart is broken too, you can't give your mother the love and compassion she needs, and she can't give you the love and compassion you need, and therefore you're angry."*

The daughter said not another word and immediately got up and moved to another seat. She didn't like what I had to say and to be honest, neither did I. What I had witnessed was the reality of people. All her mother needed was a little time to mourn. A time that she could be alone at her dinner table set for two. I don't know why, but I didn't have much compassion for the daughter. Maybe it was because not only did her mother lose her husband, but the daughter lost her father, and she didn't seem to care. Then I kept thinking about the child in me who walked out into an abandoned housing development and was ready to end my life so I could see my father again. And here was a daughter that got to spend her lifetime with her father, and she didn't seem to mourn him for more than a minute.

As I was sitting in the chair I reached into my purse and pulled out my Appointments with God notebook and without so much as a thought I began to scribe...

For the wife who is missing her husband, Love Gina.
The day comes in our life when we find someone who brings us
happiness in everything we do.

The dreams we make, a home we build, the children that we raise.

The ups and downs of life, both good and bad mistakes.

As time goes on our house seems large,

Our children have all grown.

The good times left behind us,

Our golden years to come!

Just you and I together, together as we pray,

And then one day God calls, my better half away.

Now again I'm left, this time all by myself,

I dust the pictures of our life as I put them back on the shelf.

At night I think of only you,

The life we shared on earth.

I thank you, Lord, for giving me the time we had together,

I wouldn't change a single thing. Not a moment nor an hour.

To my husband, I miss you so. I meant it when I said, "I do!"

And I'll always set our table for two.

Written for *The Lord's Blessings*

There's a place in the Bible which reads: *"I know there is nothing better than to rejoice and do good in one's lifetime; moreover, that every man who eats and drinks sees good in all his labor, it is the gift from God."* Ecclesiastes 3:12-13

I never quite understood what that meant until I met the woman who still sets her table for two.

The man who gave me the single, white rose was right. Life is about the simple things, because one day they do become the BIG things.

Appointment Twenty-Three

"PLEASE MAKE IT SNOW"

*"See that you do not despise one of these little ones. For I tell you that
in Heaven their angels always see the face of My Father who is in Heaven."*
Matthew 18:10

It was Saturday and I was exhausted. I had just been released from the hospital that morning after being diagnosed with Lupus, and needed a little more rest, so I decided to go lie in my bed to take a nap and that's when my 8-year-old niece, Mikala Strum, came into my room, crawled in my bed and asked, *"Aunt Gina, you believe in God, right?"*

"Yes, honey. I do."

She then began asking me questions, and after twenty minutes of answering her, I said, *"Mikala, if you really want to know if God is real then why don't you ask Him?"*

Mikala thought for a moment and then she crawled up on her knees, turned towards my windowsill, placed her little fingers ever so gently between the blinds and while peeking through them she said, *"Okay God, if You're real will you make it snow?"*

Oh no! I thought. It was nearing June with temperatures in the mid-70s. I wanted to tell her to ask for something else, but I couldn't. *"Mikala, why don't you lie down with me and take a nap."* I was hoping she might forget. The two of us slept for nearly two hours, when I felt a tug at my hair, *"Aunt Gina. Are you awake?"*

"I am now. What do you want, honey?"

"Do you think God made it snow?"

"I don't know. I was sleeping. Why don't you open the blinds and look?"

Mikala slowly pulled the covers off her and turned towards the window. She hesitated for a moment, but then took her two fingers and placed them between the blinds, and taking one more look back at me... *"Go ahead,"* I said. *"You won't know unless you look."* She opened the blinds.

"Aunt Gina."

"Yes."

"Look."

Snow was falling.

The two of us sat in silence. There was no need for words. We watched until the clouds rolled away, and the sun reappeared, and when the snow had melted, Mikala, giggled, jumped down off my bed and a few moments later I could hear her outside my window repeatedly yelling, *"GOD DID IT! HE MADE IT SNOW!"*

I quickly opened my bedroom window and yelled down to her, *"Hey, Mikala!"*

"Yes, Aunt Gina."

"Don't ever forget that God made it snow for you, okay? I need you to promise because sometimes when children grow up, we forget. I never want you to forget, okay?"

She smiled at me and off she ran.

For the weeks following, Mikala would run around outside, hold her arms up to Heaven and shout as loudly as she could, *"GOD DID IT! HE MADE IT SNOW!"* I loved watching her. Then one day I happened to be in the kitchen doing dishes when I noticed that Mikala had stopped shouting. Her miracle was becoming her memory and the more I kept thinking about her memory fading the more I kept remembering my miracle.

I was five years old and was in a church, wearing a white dress, and eating cake because my mother had just got remarried. I remember moving to the desert and living on an Army base. I remember being sad because I missed my grandparents. I went from living with them to wondering where they were.

But the day I remember most was the day I was at school, playing in the playground, when all of a sudden, I couldn't breathe so I opened up the playground gate and I ran. I ran until I found a place that I thought I could hide, and all I had to do was squeeze my small, framed body through a gate and hide behind a large bale of straw, and that's what I did until I heard pow-pow-pow! It seems I had run into a shooting range unaware and was so afraid I pushed my way back out the gate I had entered and ran as fast as I could.

I ran until my legs could run no farther and when I stopped there was nothing there but sand. For as far as I could see was sand, and without being afraid, I decided I would build me a house. So, I got busy. I found a piece of a broken branch, and then I drew a rectangular box in the sand. Within that box I drew a kitchen, two bedrooms, a bathroom, and a living room and when my house was completed, I stood there.

To this day I still don't know how long I was out there, but I remember I was looking one way and then I turned to look behind me, and when I did, there He was.

There was a man I had never seen before. He said nothing to me. Not a word, but I knew I was supposed to follow Him, so I did. When we finally arrived at my home, I ran into my house and when I turned to close the front door He was gone.

Time went by and it was Sunday and my friend invited me somewhere. I had no idea where we were going, but when we arrived, we were at my school. I remember being puzzled because it wasn't a school day, so not knowing what to do I followed her. But just as we were going in to sit down, I noticed a picture that was leaning against the chalkboard, so I walked up to see who it was. As I was standing there staring at this man's face, a woman walked up behind me, patted my head, and asked, *"Honey do you know who that is?"*

"No. What's His name?" I asked.

"Jesus. His name is Jesus," she said.

"Oh, that's His name." I replied.

Funny how at that moment I was so excited to know His name, and I remember telling the woman that He had walked me home the day I had run away, and all she said was, *"That's nice. Now, don't ever tell anyone else and go sit down and be quiet."*

So, I did.

Nearly twenty years have passed now since God blessed Mikala with snow and fifty years have passed since Jesus walked me home and here, I've sat quietly, not telling anyone.

It was a Tuesday, and I was sitting in my office, thinking about that day, and wondering...

So, I looked up to Heaven and asked, *"God, did Jesus walk me home that day? I need to know. I know that He did, but the few people I've told don't really believe me. Will you simply verify my miracle, just as I'm able to verify Mikala's miracle? Will You be my witness?"*

A moment later my phone rang, and it was my mother, *"Gina, I'm cleaning out my drawers and I found a few things that belong to you. Before I throw them away, I'd like you to make sure that you don't want them."*

A few days later I showed up at her house, walked into her room and there was a manila envelope lying on her bed and as I opened the envelope, I couldn't believe it. There it was. God verified my miracle. He was my witness.

That day when I was five and saw the picture of the man who walked me home, that was the only time I had ever gone to Sunday school as a child, and the picture I was looking at was a craft that we made. I had no idea that we made a picture of Jesus, framed with popsicles sticks, because my mother had taken the picture and put it away, but God in His wisdom knew that one day, five decades later, my heart would need verification of the picture of the man who walked me home. I held that

picture for at least 15 minutes and then I turned it over and there it was. My name. God knows my name.

It's interesting to me how Jesus said, *"Let the little children come to Me and do not hinder them, for to such belongs the kingdom of Heaven."* Matthew 19:14

What's even more interesting to me is only seven years after Jesus walked me home, I seemed to forget about Him, and through my hurt I wanted to end my life. Now all I want to know is why is the truth harder to believe than what the world wants us to believe.

Appointment Twenty-Four

"I FORGAVE GOD"

"Blessed are those who mourn,
for they shall be comforted."
Matthew 5:4

It was Friday when I was at work and the phone rang, *"Hello,"* I answered.

For a moment all I could hear was a young boy trying to say something. This young voice was so emotionally distraught that it took me a moment to recognize that the voice belonged to my son, *"Glenn, is that you?"*

He was crying so hard on the other end of the phone that I had to wait until he was able to breathe and then I heard, *"MOM!"*

"What's wrong, Glenn? Please tell me you're okay!"

"Mom, Kyle passed away."

"I'll be right home," I said.

As I was driving home, I began to reflect on my first  meeting with Angie, Kyle's mother. Both of our sons played on the basketball team, and both hardly ever played, so the two of us would talk. We'd talk until one of our sons was on the court and then after they were back on the bench, we'd resume our conversation. Angie and I had so much in common. We both lived on a farm, raised numerous animals, always drove around with hay in the back of our trucks, and we both had BIG, curly, hair — but more importantly... both of our sons were born in April and were only a few days apart.

I cried my whole drive home, and when I walked through my front door my son was waiting for me. He shared with me that Kyle had cancer and not many people knew about it. They just knew he wasn't at school because he wasn't well. I had no idea.

It was Tuesday, several months later, when Angie came to my house for a visit. I wasn't expecting her, so I invited her in and listened to the broken heart of a mother. I had experienced many things within my life, but to me... the loss of a child... there is nothing greater.

At this point in time, Angie didn't like God, and I completely understood. But, for some reason I couldn't let her leave my house without my sharing with her what I thought about God. She listened. She was pleasant. And then she was gone.

It was Wednesday and Angie stopped by my house again.

It was Thursday and Angie came again.

It was Friday and another visit.

Then on a Tuesday, several months later, I was picking up my kids from school when I heard a voice yell, *"GINA, WAIT!"* I turned to see where the voice was coming from when I saw Angie putting her daughter in the car, waving towards me, *"Hold on,"* she said. *"I have something to tell you."* I waited and then she came running towards me, and as she got a few steps away she reached her hands out for mine and said, *"Gina, I forgave God, and I wanted you to be the first person to know."*

I had experienced many moments within my life where I could feel the comfort of God, but to witness a mother who had lost her son forgive God for taking him home — that was my treasured moment.

As Angie was turning to leave, she turned back around and in a quiet voice she said, *"I forgave Him after meeting a group of mothers who also lost their children. We spent the weekend at a ministry called, 'Umbrella Ministries' and the woman who started it, her name is Daisy Catchings-Shader. They gave me this book and I was wondering if you would keep it for me until I'm ready to read it?"*

I took the book.

It was Monday, nearly a year later, when I happened to open a drawer at my desk and there I read, *Under God's Umbrella*. I opened the book to page one, and before I could finish the last chapter, I found myself reaching for my Appointment with God notebook and writing...

As I sit here quietly my thoughts are just of you.

All the things we used to say. All the things we'd do.

The dreams we'd share together.

The plans that we made.

Those memories I'll cherish.

Each and every day!

I remember thinking to myself, "that if I did it right;" you'd be with

me in the morning and home with me at night.

My words of loving kindness. My gentle touch to say,

"that I would never harm you, and love you every day!"

Then one night I heard a voice, a whisper from above.

I knew that it was sent for me, sent for me with love.

"I thank you for the job you did. Kyle made Me proud.

He came through the gates of Heaven, running through the crowd.

On the day that Kyle was born, I wrote his birthday down,

but not the day that you gave birth — the day I'd bring him home.

The day you held him in your arms, I saw the love you had.

I couldn't wait to hold him too, but it wasn't time... not yet!

It's hard when you love someone to ever let them go,

but know deep within your heart, I also love him so.

Kyle stands right here with Me, and someday soon you'll see.

The greatest gift I gave to you...

Now, you share with me!

We will forever be with you until you're here with us

and every time you need to, just look to us above.

Kyle hears your every prayer.

He smiles down with love.

Just listen to your heartbeat.

It's our song from up above."

Written for *The Lord's Blessings* for my friend, Angie Montre

To learn more about Umbrella Ministries visit www.umbrellaministries.com

Appointment Twenty-Five

"COLUMBINE"

"The LORD is near to the brokenhearted
and saves the crushed in spirit."
Psalm 34:18

It was Tuesday morning, and I was down at the barn milking our goats when I looked up, and through our barn window, I could see a trail of dust following my son as he was running towards the barn. When he arrived to where I was, he said through his labored breath, *"Mom, you're not going to believe this. I was watching the news, and two kids went on a rampage at a high school called Columbine in Colorado and they have no idea how many kids have been hurt, or even worse. KILLED!"*

"What?" I replied.

"Can you believe that? That's so sad. You must come up to the house and watch the news!"

I ran up to the house and I too could not believe what I had just witnessed within the world. At that moment I remember thinking... Is this the beginning of the end?

It was Friday of that week, and I was in the shower, when I heard God say, *"I want you to make comfort quilts for the families of each of the victims of Columbine."* I then looked up to Heaven and said, *"I can't do that, and besides... I wouldn't know how to get them to the families."*

I got out of the shower and went about my day. In the afternoon I had to stop at a little shop in our small town called "We Believe." This shop was owned by two sisters, Lori Lore and Kim Malarae, and each week they would faithfully order comfort quilts for their store, because they too "believed" in comfort. It seemed that after Pat had passed away, the orders just kept coming in for comfort quilts, and in memory of Pat... comfort was getting delivered.

So that afternoon, as God would have it, I stopped to deliver a comfort quilt they had ordered, but when I arrived, they were closed, and that was so unusual because they were never closed. So, I continued onward with my day.

My last stop of the day happened to be at the Penn Valley Chamber of Commerce and as I was leaving, I heard footsteps running behind me and then, *"HEY! HEY LADY!"* I turned around and said, *"Are you talking to me?"*

"Yes," said the out of breath man, *"Are you the lady that made Pat the quilt that her husband was holding at her Celebration of Life?"*

"Yes. Why?"

"Because we're getting ready to send care packages to each one of the families of those who lost a child at Columbine, and we were trying to figure out how to find you. We thought the quilts would be comforting to the families. Is there any way you can get me one so I can show our board of directors?" He asked.

At that moment I opened my car door, reached in for the undelivered quilt, and said, *"Here."*

The man turned and ran back into his building, and while I waited for him to return, I couldn't help but think, Of course Lori and Kim were not in their store. Had they been there I would not have had the quilt, and the two sisters were women of faith so of course they would lock their door if God asked them to.

Within a few moments the man returned and said, *"We love this quilt. Please deliver 13 quilts to us by Monday."*

"Are you kidding me? It's Friday. I'd have to cut out nearly 200 squares of fabric. I have to write on each quilt square... oh my gosh... that's 91 quilt squares I have to write on. Then sew them together. How can I do that by Monday???"

"Okay then. We'll give you until Tuesday."

It was Saturday and I drove up to our local Ben Franklin's and purchased 13 yards of white cotton fabric, 62 yards of variegated cotton prints, batting, and thread. When I arrived home, I cut the fabric into 12-inch squares, found the verses that God inspired my heart to place within the squares, and then I handwrote on 91 of the squares.

Sleep never appeared.

It was Sunday and when I arrived at church, I asked my pastor, Pastor Mc-Guffee, if he would announce that I needed women who liked to sew. Anyone who knew how to thread a needle was welcome at my home at 9:00am the next morning, and coffee and cake would be provided. He graciously made an announcement and on Monday, the following day, I allowed my daughters to stay home from school... the three of us waited to see who would show.

One by one ten women arrived.

Eight showed up to sew, one showed up to cook, and when the tenth woman arrived, I knew what she came to do.

"Gina, I'd like to sew the quilt for the family of Kyle Velasquez. Would that be okay?"

"Of course. Are you okay?" I asked.

Angie had lost her son Kyle to cancer and from one mother to another, Angie grabbed her sewing machine and the quilt squares, and then within the silence of her tears, she sewed each stitch with the most unspeakable love. Within a few hours 11 of us completed the quilts for: Cassie Bernall, Steve Curnow, Corey DePooter, Kelly Fleming, Kyle Velasquez, Daniel Mauser, Matt Kechter, Daniel Rohrbough, Rachel Scott, Isaiah Shoels, John Tomlin, Lauren Townsend, and Coach Dave Sanders.

It was after they were completed when I pulled out the two unsewed quilts and asked, *"Well ladies. We have two more quilts to make if you're up for it. The boys' parents who caused this pain and suffering are going to need comfort too."*

Without saying a word, each woman pitched in, and by the end of the afternoon we had completed 15 quilts.

It was Tuesday, the following day, when my phone rang and it was Angie on the other end, *"Gina, you're not going to believe this, but remember when I told you about Daisy. You know, Daisy? The woman I told you about who has the ministry for mothers called Umbrella Ministries."*

"Yes. I remember."

"Okay. Good. This morning I called Daisy, and I was telling her about the quilts that we made for the families of Columbine, and I was wondering if we could give them to her ministry and let her ministry send them?"

"Angie," I said, *"all I know is that these quilts were meant to be made and yes. I do believe that God wants you to be part of the delivery. Please come pick them up."*

A few hours later, Angie showed up at my house to collect the quilts and within the week Channel 4 News had heard about the quilts and interviewed Angie. Within the followings two weeks the quilts had travelled from Northern California to Southern California and ended up on display at Daisy Catchings-Shader's church in Palm Desert, CA.

It turned out that when Daisy's pastor heard about the quilts, he invited her to come and speak to their congregation about her ministry, and that one Sunday her ministry received more donations than they had received at any given time.

The quilts eventually made their way to the families of Columbine, but my heart believes that it was always God's intention for one to be sewn by Angie, and then be given to Daisy's ministry, because this is the way God works.

When He wants us to do something, He provides the way. I do have to share that I remember the moment in which I was getting ready to start writing on the quilt squares. That moment when I wasn't quite sure what scriptures to choose when my heart heard... *"Pick up a piece of paper and whatever I tell you to write I want you to put that in the middle square."*

The middle square on each quilt reads:

We may not understand the things that God allows.

We may not see the sunshine, breaking through the clouds.

We may not hear the whispers coming from above.

We may not know they're sent to us with love.

We may not feel the wind that soars beneath our wings.

We may not hear the angels as they loudly sing.

We may not understand the things that happen in our lives,

We may not think that life is always good and fair,

BUT God will get us through the things we cannot do!

God's in charge of everything and only HE can see you through!

Our thoughts and prayers are with you.

Written for *The Lord's Blessings* for the families of Columbine.

Appointment Twenty-Six

"GIVE IN SECRET"

"But when you give to the needy, do not let your left hand know what
your right hand is doing, so that your giving may be in secret.
And your Father who sees in secret will reward you."
Matthew 6:3-4

It was a Tuesday, and I had just been released to go home from the hospital, and as my husband was driving us up the driveway, I happened to notice that fresh flowers had been planted in one of our empty flower beds, *"Hey, did you plant those flowers while I was in the hospital?"* I asked my husband.

"Nope! Wasn't me."

When I got out of the car I smiled, walked down to where the flowers had been planted and then stood for about 15 minutes enjoying my newly planted bouquet of soon-to-be fragrance.

When my children came home from school I said, *"Hey kids. Thank you so much for planting those beautiful flowers near the fence. How thoughtful."*

I can still remember them looking at each other wondering if they should take credit for the gift when Heidi said, *"Mom, I didn't plant them."*

"I didn't plant them either," replied Shae.

"Sorry mom. I didn't even notice them," declared my son.

Weeks went by and I still had no idea who had planted my flowers. I sort of had an idea, but then I got to the place where I liked the secret of the gift. I loved going outside each afternoon to water them and watch as they grew. I simply loved the secret of my garden.

Then a few more weeks went by, and I couldn't get over how much my flowers had grown. They were now blooming, and they had become my most prized possession.

Then it happened.

It was a Thursday evening when I drove to the grocery store and as I was walking through the cookie aisle, I ran into my dear friend Angie. I loved seeing her and was always in awe of her newfound love for God. Here it had only been a few years since she had lost Kyle, yet her heart was so full, and she was always so happy.

"Hey Angie, what's up?"

"Hey Gina. I wasn't going to ever say anything, but I just have to know if you liked my gift?"

I remember the moment she said the word, "gift" I immediately thought of the secret that lied within my garden and for a moment I wished she never said anything... *"Oh, are you the one that planted the flowers?"* I asked. *"I thought it was you, but..."*

"Oh, Gina. I'm sorry. I didn't mean to spoil the gift, but I was just really hoping that you liked them."

"I loved them. Thank you so much!"

We hugged. I drove home and the minute I drove up my driveway I noticed that my flowers were wilting. They were no longer standing at attention, but more like their secret had been shared and they knew it. It was amazing.

The next morning, I poured myself a cup of coffee, placed my robe around my shoulders and forgetting my slippers, I tip-toed down to my flowers and when I arrived, I had no words.

ALL MY FLOWERS WERE DEAD!

At that moment I looked up to Heaven and asked, *"Why did my flowers have to die? What do you want me to understand?"*

And that's when my heart heard *"I put it on Angie's heart to tell you so that you would always remember what Matthew was sharing."*

I immediately ran into my house, grabbed my Bible, turned to Matthew, and read until I found... *"Be careful not to practice your righteousness in front of others to be seen by them. If you do, you will have no reward from your Father in Heaven. So when you give to the needy, do not announce it with trumpets, as the hypocrites do in the synagogues and on the streets, to be honored by others. Truly I tell you, they have received their reward in full. But when you give to the needy, do not let your left hand know what your right hand is doing, so that your giving may be in secret. Then your Father, who sees what is done in secret, will reward you."* Matthew 6:1-4

Then my heart heard, *"When I ask you to do something for another take no credit for what I ask you to do. This way the person can receive MY blessing of the gift. Do you understand?"*

"Yes, I actually do."

I then walked back down to my flowers, bent down, and pulled the dead flowers from the ground, threw them over the fence, and watched as my goats ran towards me to see what savory treat, they were being given, and it was at that moment when I realized that the flowers were not the gift.

The gift was the secret that grew from within my garden and God used Angie's giving heart to deliver the message.

APPOINTMENT TWENTY-SEVEN

"THE LORD MADE HER SMILE"

"Strength and dignity are her clothing,
and she smiles at the future."

Proverbs 31:25

Convalescent hospitals are not for people waiting to die, but rather for people with lives who are dreaming of their past, present, and future. Time — a thing of the past! I often wondered why God would allow His elderly to be placed in a solitary room, where they sit and wait for their meals, meds, baths, and prayerfully visitors.

Lessons... I used to go to the convalescent hospital to visit my husband's grandmother, Rosie. Rosie lived alone after the death of her husband and when her family moved to Northern California, she followed. Rosie was completely self-sufficient, well into her 80s, when a stroke left her paralyzed on one side and she was unable to tend for herself. Requiring 24-hour care, she needed to be placed in a room where medical attention could be provided. All her belongings were put into storage and all that was needed would be some personal items, three meals a day, and a comfortable bed to retire.

A blessing to me was that even though the stroke left her handicapped and, at times confused, she had wonderful days. Days when her mind was young, and her heart anticipated our next visit, where she would continue telling me stories about the wonderful moments that transpired from her life.

The stories she shared of her family and growing up in a family of ten children, staying married to the same man for 60 years. Never being able to afford a home, but grateful for the roof over her head. Never learning how to drive yet loving everywhere she went, and when I'd walk into her room her smile would immediately charm even my worst day.

Rosie taught me that all men are the same and that beauty comes from within. She reminded me that age is a place in your mind and that life is something so many people waste. While many of us spend our days making money, Rosie spent her days making memories. She was always dressed and ready to go in the event an opportunity would arrive.

Rosie seemed to teach me more while she was alone than she ever did when her life seemed "normal." I learned to make time for her when I had no time. I learned to listen when I used to talk. I learned not all progress is good, but sometimes destroys that which was good. I learned that life never changes unless people choose to change, and no matter how old people become... dreams never die. Dreams just get bigger (with extra time to dream).

April 9 was a Wednesday when I went to visit Rosie at her convalescent hospital. As I walked into her room, I noticed she wasn't feeling her usual self. She didn't want me to leave her or have me do her nails, which she normally loved. All she wanted was a black cup of coffee, but she was too shaky to hold it herself. I would hold the cup while she sipped, telling me how wonderful the fresh aroma of coffee was and how she'd been "sippin'" coffee for more than 60 years. Almost as if to tell me... good things still existed within the world.

Being that I was visiting on my lunch break, the hour seemed to fly by, and I had to leave. I gave her my usual kiss on her cheek and while putting lotion on her hands I said, *"Now, Rosie. I know you want to finish this cup of coffee, but it's still hot. I'm going to put the coffee on the nightstand — look here. I don't want you to touch it. It's still hot. I will tell your nurse to come in and she can help you finish it. Do you understand me?"*

She nodded, and I gave her one last kiss and a squeeze, notified her nurse and off to work I went.

A person has an interesting way of knowing one's destiny, which I believe is God's spirit who whispers... *"It's time."* The one thing I always take for granted, (coffee) Rosie seemed to savor as if she knew it would be her last cup. That evening after work I returned to the convalescent hospital because I wanted to check on her, and as I entered her room the room was cleaned, bed was made, and all her personal belongings were removed, *"OH MY GOSH, WHERE IS MY ROSIE???"*

"Gina, didn't you hear?"

"NO!!!"

"Right after you left, Rosie fell out of her wheelchair. She crushed her right leg and is bleeding internally so they took her to the hospital. I'm sorry, honey. She won't be coming back to us."

I rushed to the hospital and there we were again. Because of her age, an existing health condition and not being able to withstand the surgery, the decision was made to let her die as painlessly as possible. Another hospital. Another bed, and when she could no longer speak, she continued to teach me the value of life.

Thursday morning, I arrived at the hospital at 8:00am. Our visit lasted six days. Her hospital room became the place where God could share His miracles and I would listen. The pain and suffering that Rosie had to go through was a personal moment between Rosie and God, only He allowed me to witness part of it.

Friday she was still able to talk, but she only shared the pain she was in. For hours I would pray for God to take her home, not understanding that He was working in her life and that He needed more time.

God had made an appointment with her, and it was His time and her season. As the day progressed, and the pain still seemed to be evident, my mother-in-law and I began talking about how neither one of us knew if she really knew Christ. Rosie thought that if she talked about her salvation and accepted Christ into her heart then God might take her home sooner than she wanted to go.

At that moment I felt like I was on the phone again with Sharon's friend and remembered how she felt not knowing if Sharon understood the simplicity of salvation and it dawned on me that even though God showed me the importance of asking... because I loved Rosie so much, I never wanted to upset her, so I avoided the subject and here I was... wondering, was she saved?

In the hospital my mother-in-law and I took turns reading her the Bible and praying. We'd pray for her salvation, but knew it was something that she needed to do. We couldn't do it for her.

The last words Rosie ever said were, *"Jesus, help me!"* and she went into a coma that would last another five days.

When Saturday arrived, the day seemed to fly by. I'd just massage her hands with lotion and read the Bible. I believe at this point I was reading, and God was speaking to both of us. Nurses would come in and ask questions about what I was reading and then they would go back to their work. Some didn't understand my staying by her side, but they knew I wouldn't leave until she did. Rosie didn't want to die, so I wasn't going to let her die alone and that was that! Rosie gave her time to me and now my time belonged to her and with each passing hour I watched in amazement how her facial expressions would change and with each breath she took she looked less and less like the woman I knew.

The night was long, listening as if each breath would be her last. Sunday my husband came to visit. His parents were there, and their pastor and we all started talking about our uncertainty of her salvation and how watching her go without knowing in our hearts that she chose to be saved was very hard, when their pastor asked if we could all silently pray. We thanked him and each of us bowed our heads.

I was sitting next to her, holding her hand, and when I was done praying, I opened my eyes, and I couldn't believe what I had witnessed. She was smiling. The woman who just a minute before I no longer recognized... she looked 50 years younger. She looked so much like the woman I had heard so much about, but never personally met.

Immediately everyone was standing over her, smiling. As we all began to gather back into our chairs, we noticed that their pastor was no longer in the room. My mother-in-law immediately went to find him and when she returned, she returned alone, crying. The prayer that her pastor had prayed went like this, *"Lord, I don't normally pray for miracles that I can see specifically, but there's a family in this room that loves this woman dearly and they are uncertain of her salvation. If possible, if Rosie is going to be with You shortly, can You please make her to smile?"*

Her smile changed my life. For the rest of the afternoon the thought that God had made her smile was a miracle. How much does God have to do for me to know that He's there?

Yet He continued to talk to me.

On Monday morning my mother-in-law came in before she went to work to sit with Rosie and I went down to the cafeteria for a breather. As I was leaving, I decided I would purchase a glazed donut — something I rarely ever eat. When I returned up to Rosie's room, my mother-in-law left, and it was just the two of us again. Later in the afternoon I decided it was time to put lotion on her skin and I noticed how dry her skin had become. It was almost as if she had been burned and her skin was peeling so I looked up to Heaven and asked, *"Father God, please take her home."*

In the evening I got hungry and remembered my donut, so I grabbed it off the nightstand, and broke it into two pieces. As I went to take a bite, I happened to be looking at Rosie's skin, but as the donut reached up to my eye level, I noticed something... the glaze on my donut that was once smooth became cracked the moment it was broken in half. As I thought about that I looked over at Rosie's skin and noticed that her skin resembled the glaze on my donut and at that moment I heard this quiet voice say, *"Remember... while they were eating, Jesus took bread, and when He had given thanks, He broke it and gave it to His disciples, saying, 'Take and eat; this is My body.'"* Matthew 26:26, I couldn't breathe.

I understood exactly what He meant.

Tuesday came and went. My mother-in-law came in the evening because she wanted to stay the night with me and while we were talking, she asked, *"Gina, are you okay?"*

"I haven't said anything to anyone," I said, *"but I wonder if I did this to her? They told me she fell after I left. I knew she wanted the rest of her coffee, but I should have thrown it away. I think she was reaching for it and that is when she fell and I..."*

I couldn't stop crying. My mother-in-law let me cry and when my tears turned to sniffles, she said, *"You didn't cause her to fall. Maybe she was reaching for God."*

We didn't say another word and I fell asleep. Around 2:00am I started gasping for air and my mother-in-law came around to my chair, *"Gina! Gina! Wake up!"* she said.

"Everything is okay," I quietly said, *"I just talked to Rosie. I was walking through the forest, and I heard her voice calling me, so I went running towards her. When I was standing before her, I didn't know what to say. She grabbed me and hugged me so tightly and whispered into my ear, 'Gina, it wasn't your fault. I wasn't reaching for the coffee. I love you. I'm leaving. I'll see you soon.'"*

Then I fell back to sleep. In the morning when I awoke, I told my mother-in-law that I had talked to her, and she said, *"I know. I was awake when suddenly both you and Rosie started to gasp for air at the same time. It frightened me, so I ran to you, and half-awake, this is what you told me..."* Then reaching for a piece of paper she read, *"'Gina, it wasn't your fault. I wasn't reaching for the coffee. I love you. I'm leaving. I'll see you soon.' I didn't want to forget so I wrote down exactly what you said. I believe God allowed her to comfort you."*

Wednesday afternoon, as I was holding Rosie's hand, I turned my face towards the window and felt the warmth of the sun. I was thinking about how God allowed her to say goodbye and calm my broken heart when suddenly I felt her hand shift. It let go and when I looked over to her, she was gone.

On April 15, at 3:50pm in the afternoon, Rosie went home to be with our Father, and I left to go be with my family.

As I was driving home, I pulled my car over, grabbed my appointment book out of my purse and began to write...

A woman laid upon her bed, so much left — left unsaid.

No more words would be shared just time to sit and wait,

For the Lord to call her home, a time to meet her fate.

She was quiet, her skin was dry. Her body was dying before my eyes.

Then the Lord spoke to me, and this is what He said,

"Break this bread in remembrance of me." I knew exactly what He meant.

"This bread is My body;" I could see it with my eyes. How much more

do I need to know that God is always by my side?

And even in death do I know His words are true.

Now she laid her soul to sleep,

She blessed the Lord her soul to keep,

And since she died before she woke,

She blessed the Lord her soul to take.

Goodbye Rosie, I'll see you soon.

Written for *The Lord's Blessings*

"For God so loved the world that He gave His one and only Son, that whosoever believes in Him shall not perish but have eternal life." John 3:16 The Lord not only took Rosie home, He made her smile when she saw Him.

In Nevada City, CA, located at Hooper and Weaver Mortuary, there is a grave which reads: THE LORD MADE HER SMILE!

Appointment Twenty-Eight

"THE GARDEN"

"The Lord God took the man and put him in the
garden of Eden to work it and keep it."
Genesis 2:15

There are some things in life I can always depend on. Taxes, death, no extra money at Christmas, dogs jumping on me when I'm dressed and ready to go to work, and this little garden up the road that reminded me that another season had arrived.

Living in the country I became to depend on the seasons. The grass would come up in the spring and that would help feed our cows; summer nights allowed us to work outside longer, and we would always have an abundance of tomatoes. The fall would bring our winter harvest, and winter rains would bring me back indoors where I could finally get my house in order.

My favorite seasonal reminder always arrived in the spring through a little garden that resided on Bitney Springs Road, in Nevada City. Every year I could depend on one day simply driving by and seeing this garden getting tilled, and then I was reminded that it's time for me to plant my seeds. If I happen to drive by later and see things growing, then I immediately would panic knowing that I wasn't paying attention and missed the spring. I also knew I could no longer plant seeds but must head to the nursery and plant someone else's seeds that they nurtured.

It was Sunday, and my children and I were heading to church when I happened to drive by my favorite garden, and I noticed something different. Summer had come and gone, and the garden was left untouched, so I said, *"Hey, did any of you notice the garden by Bitney Springs?"*

"No, why?" my son asked.

"I don't know. As we drove by, I just felt as if something was wrong. When I get the chance, I'm going to stop by and introduce myself and see if everything's okay."

When I arrived at church, I asked everyone in my Bible study if they noticed the garden and everyone seemed to know which garden but didn't seem to notice the change.

Each day I would drive by the garden and notice it was still untouched. Weeks went by and I'd think, one day I'm going to stop and ask if everything is okay. Months went by and I'd think, one day I'm going to stop and ask if everything is okay. Then another summer arrived only this time I drove by the house, and I heard the Lord say, *"STOP so you can see what's wrong!"*

I happened to be passing by the house and I looked up to Heaven and said, *"I can't stop now. I must be somewhere, but one day I'm going to stop and ask if everything is okay."*

I then passed the corner of where it would have been safe to turn around and drove to where my car would need to stop. There was a three-way stop sign and not a great place to make a U-turn, so I justified the difficulty in turning back, and that is when it happened. A truck carrying a load of hay was turning to make a left-hand turn, when the truck directly in front of him ran the stop sign and hit him perfectly, knocking all his hay to the roadway. Everyone was safe, but it was there that I realized I couldn't turn right or left. I had to turn back.

And, knowing the great lengths that God will go to when He asks one to do something I stepped out of my car and yelled, *"Sorry!"*

The two men in the vehicles looked at me like, what is she sorry for? But I knew. I had nowhere to go but back, and had I listened those two men might just be headed in different directions.

Monday morning at 10:30am I turned my car around and making a left I slowly turned into the driveway of the home that tended to the garden. When I got out of my car, I noticed a body hunched over in the corner of the garden. At first, I didn't think the person would acknowledge me. The person was wearing a large hat that seemed to be larger than the body that was wearing it. *"Excuse me,"* I said.

Slowly the hat lifted and using her right arm she reached for the fence behind her to support her balance. It took her minutes to find her legs and when she did, she slowly approached me, but before she stopped, I noticed her face and without thinking I said, *"Oh my gosh. Your husband died, didn't he?"*

"How did you know and who are you? I don't know you. Why are you here? What do you want?"

All I could say was, *"I love your garden, and my heart knew it was missing something; I just didn't know it was missing someone."*

The minute I said that she reached up and took off her large hat and as her eyes filled with tears she said, *"This morning I woke up and felt so alone, so I prayed for a friend. Since my husband died, I've been quite lonely, but now you're here. You're my friend that I asked God for. Would you like to come in and have some tea?"*

The two of us slowly walked into her home. She put on the water for the tea, and we sat down on her couch. *"Hello, my name is Sofia,"* and pointing to her right she continued... *"you will find my husband's picture on the mantle. Wasn't he handsome? We met in WWII. He was a pilot, and I was a nurse. I'm from Italy. My husband was shot down and the moment I saw him at the hospital I knew I had to put him back together if I was going to marry him. We had two children and were married for 60 years."* She continued sharing about their life together and then she said, *"Please follow me."*

I followed her and she took me to a couch that had six photographs on it. There were two children that had taken three separate photographs at different ages. The first photos were taken when they were about five years of age, the second photos when they were around 12, and the last set of photos showed them to be well into their 20s.

The only problem was she knew the names of the children when they were five but couldn't seem to remember the names of the other four children. It was then that I noticed that she probably had dementia, so I acknowledged how beautiful the photos were and then she said, *"Now, that we are best friends I want to show you something. Please, follow me."*

I followed closely behind her, and she took me down a dark hallway and then reached into her pocket and pulled out a key. As she was unlocking the door to the room, she smiled at me and said, *"This is the room where my husband died. I haven't been in here since his death, but I want to show you something."*

As I walked in the door, I noticed the sweetest little bedroom. The bed was perfectly made, and their wedding photograph was erected on their little nightstand in front of a lampshade that needed to be dusted. I could tell she hadn't entered the room from the dust, and as I was looking around, I heard... *"Hello. Over here."* She pointed to her dresser and said, *"Please help me and open the bottom drawer."*

I reached down and slowly opened it and when I did my heart stopped, *"Sofia, how much money do you have in this drawer?"*

"I know. It's a lot. My kids don't know it's here. It's our life savings. I'm afraid the bank will take all my money, so I placed it all here."

My heart started to race, and I knew why God had put it on my heart to pay attention to her garden and why He needed her to pray for a friend. He needed to wait for her to ask for help so that when help arrived, she would let me in. He needed me to notice her garden so when He needed me to be her friend I would go.

To think... I almost didn't stop!!!

It was Tuesday and I came back to the house and as I was knocking on her door a woman cracked the door open, *"Hello, is Sofia here?"* I asked.

"Who are you? Why are you here?" she asked with frustration.

I motioned for her to come outside and when I did, she reluctantly put half her body out the door and said, *"Really, who are you and why are you asking for Sofia?"*

I told her who I was and then I politely asked her who she was, because I needed to know before I told her about the thousands of dollars, I had been a witness to, "*I'm her nurse. I take care of her Tuesday through Saturday and I've been here since her husband died. She has no friends, and her kids live back east so why are you here?*"

I explained to her what transpired from the day before and with tears in her eyes she said, "*I've never been allowed to go into that room. I didn't know she had a key. She always said it was locked and it needed to stay that way. Thank you so much for letting me know. I will call her daughter, now.*"

It was Thursday, and as I was driving by Sofia's house, I noticed that she was standing in her garden wearing a jacket and holding her purse. I also noticed a moving van in her driveway and boxes had already been packed. I pulled over and simply looked at Sofia and she looked back at me. For a moment she smiled and then her smile went away. I'm not sure she remembered me, but I was happy when I heard, "*Mom. Come on. It's time to go.*" Sofia was no longer alone.

I then drove away and when I got up to the three-way stop sign, I pulled off the road, reached into my purse, grabbed my appointment book, and began to write...

THE GARDEN
Everyday I'd drive by the garden near the road —
I'd see a couple gardening, green grass freshly mowed, I knew the love
between these two took years to be sowed.
I also knew the seasons by the way the garden looked.
Winter, there was nothing...
Spring, the color green...
Summer would bring the harvesting, most of the work...
Then in the fall the leaves would die to fertilize the earth!
Then one summer day, just before fall, I noticed that the garden
was not the same at all.
The story it was sharing was one that I would hear —
A story of a garden that was missing someone dear.
Then I heard a voice say, "STOP to see what's wrong."

I pulled into the driveway, and this is what I saw...
A woman in her garden sitting all alone —
Then I knew what happened. The Lord had called him home.
The garden that was shared by two now belonged to one.
And as she spoke, I listened. Our friendship had begun.
All because I noticed her garden had gone undone.
Written for *The Lord's Blessings*

Appointment Twenty-Nine

"THE BLESSED BIRD"

"Every good gift and every perfect gift is from above,
coming down from the Father of lights, with whom
there is no variation or shadow due to change."
James 1:17

It was a Saturday morning in November when Lisa stopped by my house for coffee. Lisa Newman and I met through a mutual friend when I first moved to Northern California, and from the moment we met, she became my best friend and eventually my business partner, *"Gina, I was at the Chamber of Commerce last night and they are doing a Christmas tree fundraiser."*

"What's a Christmas tree fundraiser?" I asked.

"It's where they get businesses to donate a Christmas tree, decorate the tree, and then people bid on the trees, and the highest bidders gets to take home a tree."

"That sounds like fun."

"I knew you would love it so we're going to do it, and we're going to decorate the whole tree in white doves. I have hundreds of white doves and the tree will be beautiful. I will take care of all the decorating and all you have to do is write a story that goes with white doves and a Christmas tree."

"Okay," I said, and we went back to drinking our coffee.

Then it happened.

A few weeks had gone by and as I was walking out the door to go to work, Lisa called me, *"Hey, how's that bird story coming along?"*

"I'm working on it!"

"Great." Lisa said, *"I'll need it in two days."*

"Okay, when I get home from work today, I'll finish the story up!"

I then hung up the phone and my heart began to race. I had nothing and now I had to come up with a story within two days and I had no idea how I was going to do that, so I got in my car and headed to work. Then it happened... As I was driving up Hwy 20, I looked to my left and there stood one of the tallest pine trees I had ever seen and for some reason I decided I would pull off the highway and look at it.

As I was staring at its beauty I reached into my purse, grabbed my appointment book, my trusted pen, and that is when my heart heard, *"Gina, have you ever seen a pine tree right before Christmas? The trees are so high there are days when the clouds cover the tops of the trees, and it looks as if they are reaching up to Heaven. Or have you noticed the trees right after the snow falls, their fragrance is so clean and fresh it almost seems as if the forest is being reborn."* The voice continued...

"The significance of a Christmas tree can mean so many things to people. What does it mean to you?"

Well... I began to write... I remember when I was a child, and my Christmas began with the purchasing of the tree. My grandfather, Popo, lived in another town and he would wait for us to arrive. Then on Christmas Eve, the day began with the purchasing of the tree. My fondest memory of Christmas was that moment when we'd all pile into my grandfather's ol' Dodge truck and we'd head to the tree lot. The rules were we had to find the best looking tree for the least amount of money, and we got to where we stopped looking at the price tag because it didn't matter about the price. My grandfather could talk a twenty-dollar tree down to two dollars.

The easy part was purchasing the tree. The hard part was getting my grandmother to approve the tree. My grandfather wasn't allowed to take the tree out of the back of the truck until she approved it. There were many Christmases we had to return trees. How I love those memories.

Humm, trees and memories — how they seem to fit. I think what I love most about Christmas is the families it brings together. Stories being shared from one generation to another and the fresh baked smells that seem to fly out of the darkest of hallways. Christmas is not for the young at heart, but to keep hearts young. The birth of Christ... it's too bad I only celebrate His birthday once a year.

When I was done reflecting, I put my appointment book and pen back in my purse and I drove to town. When I got home that afternoon I helped the kids with their farm chores, we all came in and had dinner and when the last plate was cleaned and put away, I sat down at my computer and wrote three words: *The Blessed Bird.*

Then I sat there. I had nothing. I sat for hours. I'd write a line about a bird and a tree and then as fast as I typed, I'd find my fingers hitting the backspace button on my keyboard and within seconds my page was right back to three words... *The Blessed Bird.*

Somewhere between midnight and 1:00am, I stepped away from my computer and as I was pushing in my chair I simply said, *"I don't know what to say God, about a Christmas tree and a dove. Please help me."* I then kissed the tip of my index finger and touched the screen of my computer. That was something I had become accustomed to doing when I didn't know what to write, and then off to bed I went.

When morning arrived, I happened to be standing in my kitchen holding my mud boots with my right hand, while sipping coffee with my left, when I happened to look over at my computer and noticed something. The blank screen that I had left opened the night before was no longer blank, so I quickly let go of my boots, and ran to my computer and began reading...

The Blessed Bird
High atop a tall fir tree, higher than the eye can see — lives a gift from up above,
The Blessed Bird... The Great White Dove!
They say that on the sacred eve when Jesus Christ was born,
a fir tree grew from where appeared.
No one knew but God.

But on the top of the tree God set His eyes upon,

So, He could see the sacred birth — the birth of His newborn Son.

And everyone from far and near also came to see...

That God was doing all He'd said... filling prophecies.

As time went on and Jesus grew the blessed bird would fly.

The spirit of the Great White Dove was always by His side.

Then on the day the heavens opened, they say a spirit flew,

Into the soul of the Man God sent for me and you,

"And Jesus, when He was baptized, went up, straight out of the water;

and Lo, the heavens were open up to Him, and He saw the spirit of God

descending like a dove, and lightening upon Him." Matthew 8:16

Now legend speaks of a dove that on one special night —

Will fly a-top the tall fir trees to bless for sacrifice.

The trees are cut and brought to town so everyone can see...

That Christmas is approaching, it's almost Christmas Eve.

Now still inside of the tree, even though it's cut...

Lives a spirt of the one they call, "The Great White Dove."

A gift sent from up above,

To remember His sacred Son the one He loved so much,

That Christmas is not about what's gathered around the tree,

But rather what lives inside the hearts of you and me.

Now on the morn of Christmas Day they say a spirit flies...

Leaving peace, happiness, joy and love...

Your Christmas gift from the Great White Dove

Written for *The Lord's Blessings*

After I read the story I smiled, because I had a dream where I was back, sitting at my computer, writing. I really thought it was a dream, but God needed me to go to sleep so that He would wake me up and I'd be able to hear Him as He shared His story about what a Christmas tree means to Him. After I read, *The Blessed Bird* I picked up the phone and dialed... *"Lisa, the story that you asked for is done, and I really think you're going to love it."*

She did!

Appointment Thirty

"SLOW TO SPEAK"

"Whoever desires to love life and see good days, let him
keep his tongue from evil and his lips from speaking deceit;
let him turn away from evil and do good;
let him seek peace and pursue it."

1 Peter 3:10-11

It was a rainy Tuesday afternoon when I was sitting at my kitchen table reading... *"Know this, my beloved brothers: let every person be quick to hear, slow to speak, slow to anger; for the anger of man does not produce the righteousness of God. Therefore, put away all filthiness and rampant wickedness and receive with meekness the implanted Word, which is able to save your souls. But be doers of the Word, and not hearers only, deceiving yourselves. For if anyone is a hearer of the Word and not a doer, he is like a man who looks intently at his natural face in a mirror. For he looks at himself and goes away and at once forgets what he was like."* James 1:19-24

Quick to hear, slow to speak and slow to anger... Does anyone know such a person? I thought to myself as I was headed to the mud room to get my boots on.

The weather was sharing its presence, and before the storm arrived, I wanted to be done feeding. I was tired, cold, and irritated and all I wanted to do was feed and be done with my day and then it happened. My phone rang...

Frustration immediately set in because I had just got my mud boots on and would have to take them off to go into my house to answer the phone, so kicking them off I ran into the house and abruptly answered, *"HELLO!"*

"Hello, this is your neighbor that lives at the bottom of your property. The water from your pastures is running into my yard and I was wondering if you could do something to stop it?"

Oh sure, I thought to myself. I'll just go outside and turn the rain off. Just give me a minute.

Now, since I was quick to speak, I immediately replied, *"Right now I'm in the middle of my own crisis. My mud room is flooded and I'm up to six inches of water and it's rising as I'm speaking to you. If I have a minute, after I'm done cleaning up my own mess, I will walk down and check it out!"* Then without saying, "goodbye" I hung up the phone.

Again, I found myself back in the mud room, putting on my mud boots and the whole time I was thinking, who does this woman think she is asking me to deal with the weather?

Finally, I made it down to the barn, and as I began to walk into the goat barn, I realized that in the midst of my anger I had forgotten to grab the milking buckets. Back up to the house I stormed and with each step I took the rain stormed with me. And then it happened. As I reached to open the mudroom door, I noticed it was stuck and water was coming out from underneath so I pulled on the door as hard as I could and when the door opened a big gush of water came towards me. The mud room was completely flooded and within ¼ inch from entering my kitchen.

But how? I thought.

I was not even gone for ten minutes. How could so much rain squeeze through the back door of my mud room, rise 12 inches, and then nearly flood into my kitchen? How?

Within a moment I knew. God had allowed my mud room to be flooded so that I would have to take a minute to clean up my lie. I must admit that I stood there in shame and then reaching for my mop I caught a reflection of my face from the window that was placed within the door I had just opened, and my heart heard...

"For if anyone is a hearer of the Word and not a doer, he is like a man who looks intently at his natural face in a mirror. For he looks at himself and goes away and at once forgets what he was like." James 1:23-24

I've never experienced a moment so true in my life, because the moment I saw my face I didn't recognize myself and said out loud, *"Gina, who are you that you would create such a lie and allow yourself to talk so badly to an elderly woman? What happened to you today?"*

Before I dealt with my animals, I walked down to my neighbor's home and noticed that a large tree branch had fallen in our ditch and needed to be removed. I reached down and removed the branch, and within a moment the water was flowing in the right direction. I then looked up and I saw her standing by the window, watching me. I waved. She smiled and then she closed her curtains.

As I was walking back up to my barn to begin my chores over again God reminded me of Matthew 12:36-37, *"I tell you, on the day of judgment people will give account for every careless word they speak, for by your words you will be justified, and by your words you will be condemned."*

I now understand the value of empty words, and just how far God will go to give a Bible lesson.

Lesson learned.

Appointment Thirty-one

"MY GRANDMOTHER'S PAINTING"

"For the gifts and the calling of God are irrevocable."
Romans 11:29

Painting and writing go hand-in-hand. One is expressed with a brush and the other a pen. As I look at the paintings of others, I always try to see the story the artist is telling. Many a stroke has been guided by the desire to show the world what lies within their heart.

When I was a child my grandmother, Nanny, was always painting, and when we'd go to her house for a visit there would be a new masterpiece leaning against a wall in her home. Some I liked and then there were those that I didn't really understand.

She was diligent, too.

Every Sunday she and my grandfather would load up her masterpieces and go to the park to sell. She would always be so thrilled when she was able to sell one. The sunsets, ocean, and mountain scenes, she would erect on easels waiting for the right person to come along. A person who would be able to look beyond the colors and see what she saw, allowing her to write a story without ever having to say a word. How I loved her paintings.

Decades passed, and on a Wednesday afternoon I arrived at my grandmother's house for a visit. It had been nearly a year since our last visit, and I couldn't wait to sit at her kitchen table and listen to what she had been up to and see the paintings that I had yet to see...

"Hey Nanny, I don't see anything new. Where are all your paintings?" I asked.

"Gina, I don't paint anymore. My paints are in the hall closet. I can't see. My eyes are gone, and my arthritis won't allow me to hold the brush. I had my time to paint and now my time is over. I have tons of paintings in the back bedroom closet and before you leave, please take as many of them as you want."

I didn't know what to say so the two of just sat at her kitchen table in silence. She was looking out her kitchen window, probably reflecting on her past, and I seemed to be looking onward towards my future and all I could think of was the day when my hands wouldn't work as quickly as my mind. A time when I too would have to lock my pens in the closet and the only words that would be left by me were the words that my younger self produced, and at that moment my heart heard...

"Do not boast about tomorrow, for you do not know what the day may bring." Proverbs 27:1

Then I kept thinking about all the moments when I heard God say, "Write this down. Remember this. Share this. Do this. Stop saying you'll do this tomorrow when you don't even know if you'll have a tomorrow."

It hit me. I finally understood what God was saying. My grandmother's tomorrow had arrived, and she would no longer say, "Tomorrow I will paint."

That evening, when my grandmother was sleeping, I went into her back bedroom and opened the closet door and there were her paintings. I then decided I would take her paintings out of the closet and line them side-by-side against her living room wall and in the morning, I would surprise her.

When the morning I arrived, I put on a pot of coffee and waited for her. When I heard her footsteps coming down the hallway I smiled. I couldn't help but wonder if her paintings would take her back to the days when she was painting them, and then I saw her.

As she began to take her first step up into her kitchen she stopped and smiled. I immediately jumped up, grabbed her a cup of coffee and said, "Please follow me.

Today we are having an art show by the famous painter, Kay Misken. and here is a complimentary cup of coffee."

The two of us went into her tiny living room and as we walked by the paintings, she told me about each one, (when she painted them and why) and when we were done, she smiled and said, *"Okay. Pick one. Which one do you want? I want you to take your favorite."*

"Okay. Tonight, when you go to bed, I will decide which one I want and then when you wake up in the morning, the one I'm going to take will be the only painting left in the room. This way I will surprise you with my favorite."

When evening arrived and my grandmother went to bed, I decided that I was going to pick my selection based off a story I could write from one of her paintings, so I reached into my purse, grabbed my appointment book and with my pen in hand I began...

My grandmother's painting, she painted it herself...
And when it was complete, it sat on her shelf.
Every time I stopped by the painting I would see,
The story it was telling. A story just for me.
The house was small and painted white,
The fence was painted too.
Two bush trees grew in the yard,
The flowers that peaked were blue.
The road to the house was long and narrow,
And the old oak tree perched a sparrow.
Had leaves that would die before the snow,
And return in the spring.
Seasons would transform the house,
Like birds with their new wings.
Every time I stopped and stared; I saw more than before.
Sometimes I would even swear, I'd feel the cool wind blow.
Then one day I wondered if that house were really mine...

Would I even notice or ever take the time?
To sit and enjoy the simpler things...
Would I walk down the path?
Or run by with my life?
That painting now belongs to me,
And in my heart, it stands...
A daily reminder of how beautiful life can be.
A gift from my grandmother's hands.
Written for *The Lord's Blessings*

When I finished scribing, I realized that what I had written was not about any of the paintings I had just taken out of her closet but was about one that had been hanging in her living room since I was a kid.

When the next morning arrived, I got up and my grandmother was sitting in her living room and as I walked in, she asked, *"You don't want any of my paintings? You said you were going to pick one, but I see you put them all back in the closet."*

"Yes, I want this one."

And handing her my notebook I said, *"Please read."*

She began reading and when she was done, she got the biggest smile on her face and said, *"Take the painting off the wall and turn it over, quickly."*

I did and when I turned the painting over it read: *For Gina. Love Nanny.*

"You painted this for me?" I asked.

"Yes, when you were in high school, but you didn't seem to notice it then. I can't tell you how happy I am right now. I haven't felt like this in a very long time. I wish that I would have known when my day was going to come when I couldn't paint anymore, because to be honest... I would have painted more."

As I was driving home from my visit, I was thinking about how grateful I was that I didn't put off any of the thoughts that God had placed within my heart... Go get her paintings out of the closet... Line them up where she can remember... This is the painting I want you to write about... Let her know that she is valued. Do this today. Do this now.

I understand the value of now. Too bad my grandmother had to wait over 20 years for me to praise her work, and from now on when I value someone or what they have done I'm not going to wait 20 years. I'm going to tell them then because this is so true...

"You do not know what the day may bring forth. Let another praise you, and not your own mouth; someone else, and not your own lips." Proverbs 27:1

Note about the painting. In 2006 I was moving, and the painting got destroyed in the move, but will forever remain within my heart.

Appointment Thirty-Two

"WHAT'S IMPORTANT IN YOUR WALLET?"

"Rejoice always, pray without ceasing, give thanks in all circumstances;
for this is the will of God in Christ Jesus for you."
1 Thessalonians 5:16-18

It was a Friday when I stepped foot off the plane to catch a taxi. Destination, Loma Linda University Hospital.

I couldn't believe that my grandfather, Popo, was being stubborn and didn't want to have life-saving surgery, and that was the reason for my visit. I was going to tell him all the many reasons why he had to have the surgery, but as I walked through his hospital room door there is where I heard, *"There's my Gina. I've been waiting for you. Now I can have the surgery."*

"What?" I asked. *"I thought you were choosing not to have it!"*

"I wasn't if you didn't come, but I knew you would come, so I guess I was always planning on having the surgery and I knew you would arrive right on time."

A moment later his nurse walked in, and they wheeled him away in his bed, but as he turned the corner he said, *"I love you. I'll see you soon,"* and he was gone.

As I stood in his empty room, I decided that I would go find the hospital's chapel and wait there. The chapel seemed like the perfect place to find peace while I was waiting, so that's what I did. I walked in and there he was. Jesus was placed on the altar, next to a few Bibles and the lights were dimmed in such a way that the moment I walked in I could feel the comfort I was needing.

A few hours later, as I was walking out the chapel door, I happened to look over and noticed there was a plate filled with little baggies, holding a tiny cross and a poem that read:

THE CROSS IN MY POCKET

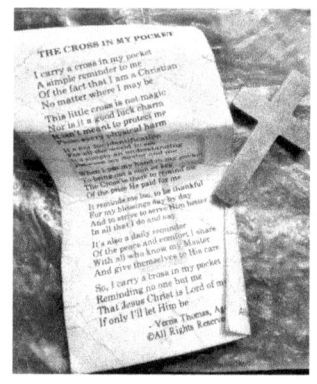

I carry a cross in my pocket

A simple reminder to me

Of the fact that I am a Christian

No matter where I may be.

This little cross is not magic

Nor is it a good luck charm

It isn't meant to protect me

From every physical harm.

It's not for identification

For all the world to see

It's simply an understanding

Between my Savior and me.

When I put my hand in my pocket.

To bring out a coin or key

The Cross is there to remind me

Of the price He paid for me.

It reminds me too, to be thankful

For my blessings day to day

And to strive to serve Him better

In all that I do and say.

It's also a daily reminder

Of the peace and comfort I share

With all who know my Master

And give themselves to His care.

So, I carry a cross in my pocket

Reminding no one but me
That Jesus Christ is Lord of my life
Only if I'll let Him be.
Written by Verna Thomas

After I read the poem, I noticed there was a sign which read: *"Take one."* So, I did. I took one and stuck it in my wallet and there it has remained now for over 24 years. There are so many days when I look back on this moment and I'm reminded of when my grandfather said, *"There's my Gina. I've been waiting for you."* I believe that's what God says about each of His children, *"There's my child... I've been waiting for you."*

Back to my appointment... The next day was Saturday when I came back to visit my grandfather, and as I walked into his hospital room the lights were dimmed and the curtains around his bed were closed. As I was getting closer, I could hear him speaking. Not completely able to hear what he was saying or who he was talking to, I quietly moved towards the curtains, and not wanting to interrupt, I gently opened the curtain, and this is what I saw...

His eyes were shut, his hands were folded in prayer, and in the quietest voice he was reciting the Lord's Prayer, and to this day, I believe I got to witness a moment between a man and his God, and when he got done, he opened his eyes. I was so emotionally moved that I neglected to move away from the curtain, *"I bet you didn't know that I knew that prayer, did you?"* he asked.

I moved in closer, and he grabbed my hand and simply told me he loved me. There was no need to talk any further. I witnessed a moment and every time I hold that little cross in my hands, I'm reminded of the simplicity of...

"And when you pray, you must not be like the hypocrites. For they love to stand and pray in the synagogues and at the street corners, that they may be seen by others. Truly, I say to you, they have received their reward. But when you pray, go into your room and shut the door and pray to your Father who is in secret. And your Father who sees in secret will reward you. And when you pray, do not heap up empty phrases as the Gentiles do, for they think that they will be heard for their many words. Do not

be like them, for your Father knows what you need before you ask Him. Pray then like this: 'Our Father in Heaven, hallowed be Your name. Your kingdom come, Your will be done, on Earth as it is in Heaven. Give us this day our daily bread, and forgive us our debts, as we also have forgiven our debtors. And lead us not into temptation, but deliver us from evil.' For if you forgive others their trespasses, your heavenly Father will also forgive you, but if you do not forgive others their trespasses, neither will your Father forgive your trespasses." Matthew 6:5-15

Appointment Thirty-Three

"THE KEYS OF LOVE"

"So now faith, hope, and love abide, these three;
but the greatest of these is love."
1 Corinthians 13:13

Every story has been given a time to be shared...

On December 17 of the year 2000, my grandfather, James Milan Misken passed away. He passed on the 7th day at the 7th hour.

As long as I can remember my grandfather was my best friend. He taught me everything from riding a bike to driving a car, and when I got married, he cried, when I moved away, he cried, and the year his mind worked better than his body, he cried. Those were the only three times I ever saw him cry.

His funeral was on a Thursday, and I cried.

My grandfather was the greatest storyteller, and it was only appropriate that he would share a story with me that I was to leave with his family.

When I was in my teens, I had a mind of my own and a spirit that needed time to be tamed. One afternoon I decided that it was time for me to pack my bags and move on. I was only 13 years old and didn't want anyone to know where I was going so, I told my siblings that I was running away, where I'd be, and then quietly left. When I arrived at my destination, I found my grandfather sitting on the bench as if he too were waiting for the bus. I tried to avoid him, but he inevitably saw me and motioned for me to come and sit beside him.

I can still remember the clothes I was wearing; white, Ditto jeans, and a red, white, and blue bicentennial tank top. I also remember how the air smelled of car fumes, and the sound of traffic was almost overwhelming as we sat there in silence waiting for one of us to speak. After a few moments my grandfather looked over at me and began, *"Gina, I am not here to bring you back home. I am here because I want to give you three things."*

I smiled and he continued.

"You and I have always been very close. Do you know why we are so close?" he asked.

"No," I replied.

"Because you've always reminded me of my three children."

He continued by saying that when parents are raising their children, they are busy. They are raising a family and have little time and then if they are fortunate enough their children will have children and they will be blessed with grandchildren. *"Grandchildren are gifts their children give to their parents,"* he said.

He continued to talk for several minutes and then reached into his pocket, *"Gina, when my Trisha was a young girl and ready to leave to be married, I had to have FAITH that she would be taken care of. I had to have FAITH that her husband would provide her with everything in life, and I had to have FAITH that I would be able to walk through the door every evening and know that she was happy. You are also the first child born to your mother, so I have to have FAITH that when you leave you will take care of yourself and be okay."* At that moment he handed me an ol' skeleton key and told me the key was a reminder of his Trisha and to carry FAITH with me wherever I may go.

He continued onward by telling me about his son Jimmy, and how Jimmy had a mind of his own and was passionate about everything. He told me that to have that much passion you have to LOVE and then he handed me another ol' skeleton key and told me that key was his reminder of Jimmy and to always remember to LOVE family, friends, and things that are important in life.

The final key he was holding represented my mother. My mother was his last child, and he hoped after raising three children that he had raised them all right, and to always remember that if there's HOPE in my heart there will always be a better tomorrow.

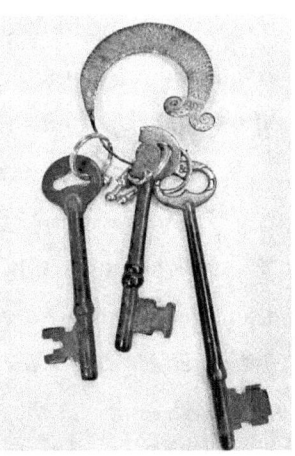

When his story was finished, we didn't say a word and I jumped into his truck and came home. It wasn't until I was getting ready to leave for his funeral that I stumbled upon the ol' keys — keys that were hidden in a shelf and when it was time, I would bring them out, dust them off, and give them back to their rightful owners.

I no longer own the keys to my grandfather's heart. At his funeral I retold his story and gave each of his children back their keys. I believe he knew I would remember the story of the keys and when he wanted to tell his children one more time how much he loved them, I would remember.

My grandfather used to tell stories to us all the time, but before he would tell us the story he would ask, *"Have you heard the story of...?"*

If we answered, *"Yes,"* he would immediately ask us to retell the story. If we couldn't remember, he would get upset and make us beg him to continue. I now believe in my heart he was just making sure that we wouldn't forget.

John F. Kennedy once said, *"One person can make a difference, and everyone should try."* How true this is for me because my life would have never been the same without this one person in it, and as long as I'm alive and able to retell his stories — his life will continue to affect others and so on and so forth.

Now, for the rest of his story...

On December 17, 1999, a year to the day before my grandfather passed away, I had come for a visit and the two of us were sitting in his family room. The room where each year we would erect the Christmas tree, and the place where we would play cards late into the night. I loved that room. Many fond memories happened between those four walls, but my greatest memory of all was on December 17,

1999. The day he looked at me, clenching his arthritic hands, and said, *"Gina, I've been telling you stories my whole life. Now, I want you to tell me a story. I want you to tell me about that Jesus you talk about all the time."*

"What do you want to know?"

"I want to know how I can meet Him someday." He answered.

I looked over at him and within the simplicity of breathing I said, *"The Bible says if you confess with your mouth that Jesus is Lord and believe in your heart that God raised Him from the dead, you will be saved. For with the heart one believes and is justified, and with the mouth one confesses and is saved. Do you believe that?"*

And then with the biggest smile, he looked over at me and said, *"I do! I believe that!"*

"Well then, you're good to go home when it's time." I said with a hug.

A moment later my grandmother Nanny, stuck her head out through the hallway and said, *"I believe that, too."*

She then excused herself and drove to The Dollar Store for some milk. When she returned, she handed me a bag, saying, *"Here, this is for you. Keep it always."* When I opened it there was a bright golden orange candle holder that read: I LOVE JESUS.

Yes, we do!

In loving memory of James Milan Misken

January 5, 1914 – December 17, 2000

Faith: *"So faith comes from hearing, and hearing through the word of Christ."* Romans 10:17

Love: *"For God so loved the world, that He gave His only Son, that whoever believes in Him should not perish but have eternal life."* John 3: 16

Hope: *"Therefore, preparing your minds for action, and being sober-minded, set your hope fully on the grace that will be brought to you at the revelation of Jesus Christ."* 1 Peter 1:13

Appointment Thirty-Four

"DO YOU KNOW WHAT
MY FAVORITE THINGS ARE?"

"He has made everything beautiful in its time. Also, He has put eternity into man's heart, yet so that he cannot find out what God has done from the beginning to the end."

Ecclesiastes 3:11

"God, grant me the serenity to accept the things I cannot change, the courage to change the things I can, and the wisdom to know the difference." Serenity Prayer

"Hello," he said.

"Hello," I replied.

"I'm Nicholas."

"Well, hello. I'm Gina."

"Would you like to know the name of my pig?" Nicholas asked.

"I would love to know the name of your pig!"

"His name is Milky Way."

"Milky Way?" I replied. *"Oh yes, I see it. He's choco-late on the outside and creamy white on the inside."*

"Yep." Nicholas smiled. *"He's, my pig. I walk him sometimes and take care of him for my brother."*

141

I just smiled as he continued... *"Do you know what my favorite things are?"*

"Nope!"

"My favorite things are my fire truck, my blanket, and my baseball trophy."

"Those sound-like wonderful things!" I said, smiling back at him.

"Yep."

A few minutes later I began talking with his mother, Jami. She was leaning against the metal gate watching her boys tag and weigh-in her oldest son, Brandon's hog for the upcoming fair, when I noticed she was not your typical 4-H mother. She was wearing pedal pushers and a light shirt. Her nails were perfectly manicured and there wasn't a hair out of place. I had to smile when I noticed she was wearing open-toed shoes, and I knew that this experience was completely new to her because most of us in the hog barn looked like we had been in the hog barn for weeks, and she represented how I felt on the inside but neglected to portray on the outside.

"Hi. I've never truly introduced myself, but I'm Gina. Your son Brandon is in my husband's swine group, and every time he has a meeting, I've been busy, but I've seen you down at the barn."

"Yes, I know," she said with laughter. *"I'm Jami. I'm the one who came to your house an hour late because I got completely lost."*

Jami and I continued to talk, and when the boys were done weighing their hog, we said our goodbyes, and off we both went in different directions.

And here is the deep breath I take where I can't seem to remember what happened between our goodbye and this moment. It seems that even though I am journaling this day from memory I can't seem to recall what I did from the moment I said goodbye to Jami until the moment we were brought back together...

...I was walking through the Nevada County Fairgrounds when I heard a voice yelling for me, *"Gina, have you seen Jami?"*

"I was with her a little bit ago, but I have no idea where she is now." I yelled back. But since his voice was filled with such urgency, I started running with him, *"Here, you go this way and I'll go that way,"* and the two of us took off running in different directions until I saw her running towards me, and then past me, and I

ran quickly behind her. I had no idea where we were running to, but we were running. I have no knowledge of how long we ran for but the next thing I know is we were standing in a near-empty campground, filled with emergency vehicles and a helicopter, and by the time we had arrived Jami's son, Nicholas (who was five years old) was laying on the stretcher being lifted into the helicopter, and that was the moment when Jami collapsed into my arms.

As I looked around, I could see many of my friends. Friends I had known for years, only at that moment I couldn't recognize their faces. Then I looked over and saw my daughter, Shae, standing alone looking like she was lost in the desert, and that was the first moment when I saw the look of shock in real-time.

A moment later Jami and I were surrounded by people and the first thing I thought was, Lord, I wish I could pray out loud because we need to pray, NOW! At that moment a young girl of maybe 17 jumped in the middle of all of us and she began praying. I don't remember her prayer, but I remember thinking her words were perfect, and I appreciated that in the midst of uncertainty there was a young girl brave enough to step in the middle of us all and pray, and she prayed until an EMT came over and told us that Nicholas was being flown to Sutter Memorial in Roseville.

At that moment I asked my friend Kathy Dorris if she would stay with Jami while I ran to get my car. Kathy didn't say a word but just held Jami up. A few minutes later I arrived, and we placed Jami in the passenger seat, and her son Brandon, and Kathy sat in the backseat. As I was getting ready to leave, I noticed my daughter Shae, and ran over to her. By the look of her face I knew that she had witnessed a moment that she would never forget. So, I grabbed her, told her I loved her and that I would be home soon. Then I yelled at all the parents I knew to watch over my daughter. I knew that she would be well cared for, just as I knew in my heart that no matter the outcome, Nicholas would be cared for as well.

When I arrived back at my car I jumped in the seat, put my seatbelt on, and just as I began to insert my key into the ignition a fireman came up to my window, bent down and looking me straight in the eyes asked, *"Do you know where you're going?"*

"*Yes,*" I replied.

"*Are you sure?*"

"*Yes, my mother-in-law was in a head-on collision a week ago and she was flown there. I know exactly where to drive Jami.*"

He then reached his head in through my car window and whispered, "*Please drive carefully. May God go with you.*"

"*He will.*"

As he went to stand back up, I noticed a tear that had snuck its way down from beneath his sunglasses. I nodded up at him, and then took a silent moment and prayed, "*Lord, I can't do this without you. Please Lord, give me the strength to drive, to not lose it, and to get Jami where she needs to be safely so she can be with Nicholas. In Jesus' name, amen.*" And with that short, quiet prayer I turned on the car's engine and off we went.

When we arrived at the offramp and proceeded onto the highway a group of high school kids drove past us, smiling and singing to whatever was playing on their radio and I thought to myself, they have no idea what the people in my car are going through. At that moment Jami and I began to talk, and it was then when it hit me that God had prepared me for this drive all week.

My car...

My car would be best described as something you could live out of if you had to, and I gamble with the amount of gas I have in the tank. It also seats five, but comfortably it only seats one. I'm always too busy to care what my car looks like, because it's always just me and my kids. But this day my car was clean, because the Wednesday before I had this great urge to clean it out and for two hours, I scrubbed the car like it had never been scrubbed before. I took my son's air compressor and blew fragments of hay outside the car, and then I vacuumed. I found the Armor All and armored all. I even went to the store and purchased Febreeze. And, because I use my car as a travelling office, I removed the bills that had piled up in my cup holder and filed them. For the first time in six months, I could see that the photo of

Jesus that Shae and I had taped in my car, was still firmly in place. Then on Thursday I went and filled up my car with gas and on Friday I asked my husband to check my tires because they seemed a tad low.

Then Sunday arrived, and it was weighing day at the fair. The one day where the kids take their fair animal to be tagged and weighed. When I got out of my bed, my husband and three children had already been outside, had fed and loaded up all their animals and were ready to go, so I yelled out our bedroom window, *"Have a good day. I'll see you when you get home."*

But as I went to close the window my heart heard, *"You need to go, too."*

The voice was so loud that I re-opened the window and yelled for them to wait, and my husband said he would, but then my heart heard, *"Let them go and you can meet up with them later."* So, I yelled again, *"No, you guys go ahead, and I'll catch up with you later,"* and off they drove.

It only took me a few minutes to get ready, grab my coffee, and out the door I went. But then something interesting happened. As I was driving down the driveway I heard, *"You didn't take your allergy medicine."* And, then I thought to myself, well that won't matter because I won't need to run today. I will be walking. But the voice was so strong that I turned my car around, walked into the house, took my medication and off I went to the fair with a clean car, a full tank of gas, and a picture of Jesus. God had prepared me for this moment.

About half an hour into the drive Jami's heart began to settle. It took everything Kathy and I had to keep her in my car. She was in such shock, and she kept wanting to open the passenger car door so she would be able to run to Nicholas. A moment I will never forget.

When we began to enter Roseville my daughter Heidi called my cell phone and said that plans had changed and that they had flown Nicholas to Sierra Nevada Memorial Hospital. Kathy had answered my cell phone, and after she hung up, she said, *"And Gina. Heidi told me to tell you that when you come home you need to stop and pick up some ice cream."*

My heart sank because ice cream was something we ate after we lost a loved one. I had always wanted to teach my kids how to celebrate the life of the one we lost, and by doing so, when we received the news of a loved one's death or of a friend, I would fix each of us a big bowl of ice cream, and we would talk about the person we were missing through a big bowl of comfort.

For a moment I couldn't breathe.

I then got off the freeway, turned around and headed to the hospital, and then Kathy told Jami that was good news that they had turned around because maybe that meant he didn't need as much medical attention as they thought. It's amazing how when a mother has something, anything, to believe in her breath will return.

It was at that moment when Jami noticed the picture of Jesus, and His presence through the photo seemed to calm her heart that much more.

As we approached the hospital, I pulled over to the curb to let the three of them out, and as I looked over at Jami, I noticed her body language had changed. The woman who first stepped into my car was not the same woman who was stepping out. She stepped into my car with her own strength and stepped out with God's.

As the three of them went into the hospital I pulled the car into a parking space and took a moment to get my breath because I knew what I would be walking in to, and when I finally made it into the hospital Kathy had me paged. When I found Kathy, she was crying, and told me that Nicholas didn't survive the accident.

"*I know,*" I said.

"*How did you know?*" she asked.

"*Heidi told me.*"

A few moments later I found myself in a dark room with Jami sitting in a hospital chair, clutching her stomach, crying uncontrollably while rocking back forth surrounded by the silence of doctors. No one said a word.

I kneeled before her, grabbed her hands, and she said, "*Gina, my baby is gone.*" I didn't say a word.

Then within her tears she said, "*I want to see him.*"

The nurse walked to the door, I grabbed Jami's hand and the two of us followed as she led us through the emergency room, to a little room on the side.

When we were inside, they brought her a rocking chair and she quietly sat in it. Then the nurse walked out, and it was just the two of us, so I picked up Nicholas and placed him gently in her arms, and within a moment the door opened, her family had arrived, and that was my cue to go and wait outside with Kathy.

Now, there are certain people who should be called angels, and Chaplain Derry James is one of them. Her job is to bring people comfort and find peace in the midst of a person's worse moment in life, and while Kathy and I were outside waiting she approached us and asked, *"I'd like to talk to you both. Jami is having a hard time letting go of Nicholas, and I was wondering if you could help me."*

"We have no idea how to help you in this situation. We're moms too, and we would never want to let our child go, so how can we help?" I asked.

Then the chaplain said this...

...*"I wish I knew what Nicholas had liked to do. I wish I knew what his favorite things were."*

"Why do you need to know that?" I asked.

"Because sometimes when someone loses someone it's a comfort for them to have some of their favorite things so that the surviving family members may feel they are not leaving their loved one alone but are leaving them with things that brought them comfort."

I couldn't believe my ears, because upon meeting Nicholas a few hours before he asked me, *"Do you know what my favorite things are?"*

"Nope."

"My favorite things are my fire truck, my blanket, and my baseball trophy."

"Those sound-like wonderful things." I said, smiling back at him.

"Yep."

Kathy and I immediately left the hospital and drove to Jami's apartment where we collected all of Nicholas' favorite things, brought them to Jami and within a moment I knew exactly what Chaplain Derry James was talking about.

Comfort had arrived.

On my way home I stopped at the store, purchased some ice cream, and then my family and I sat at our dinner table and talked about the events that transpired during the day. It was a sad day, and a day that I knew would change my life forever.

But what did I learn from the brief time that I got to spend with Nicholas?

Pondering that question, I opened my Bible, and it was here where I read, *"He has made everything beautiful in its time. Also, He has put eternity into man's heart, yet so that he cannot find out what God has done from the beginning to the end."* Ecclesiastes 3:11

But, my heart heard, *"Gina, I have made every person's life beautiful during their time, even if it's brief. Look back on the events that transpired during the week. I had you clean your car, fill its tank with gas, take your medication so you could run, and I had you remove your paper waste so Jami would be reminded that I would be with her always and forever. And, more importantly I specifically had Nicholas tell you what his favorite things were because I knew that you would listen. I know that you don't understand that there isn't anything that could change the course of what happened today, but I want you to take Nicholas with you wherever you go through-out your life because he was the most influential person you have met or ever will meet, and with time he will have taught you that nothing can change what has already been set in motion."*

Appointment Thirty-Five

"A MOMENT OF COMFORT"

*"Honor your father and your mother, that your days may be
long in the land that the LORD your God is giving you."*
Exodus 20:12

It was a Saturday evening when my family and I had stayed at my parents' house. It was the night before we would be moving from Southern California to Northern California, and my mother wasn't happy. She wasn't happy because we were relocating for my husband's job, and I was taking her only three grandchildren with us.

As I was lying in bed that night I couldn't help but wonder about a quote I had once read which shared, "Grandchildren give us a second chance to do things better because they bring out the best in us," and in my excitement of moving I wondered if I was taking away her second chance, and it was there where my excitement turned to sorrow, because I knew that one day I would want my second chance and I was taking hers away.

Then one Sunday, seven years later, I was sitting at my kitchen table, drinking a warm cup of coffee, when my phone rang, and it was my mother. She asked me how our kids were doing, and how my job was going. We talked about the normal everyday things of life, and our conversations always closed the same way, *"I miss you mom. I wish we lived closer."*

"I know, darlin'. We'll talk again soon."

But on this day, it was different, because when I hung up the phone, I realized something that I had never noticed before. I had become the woman I had remembered her to be. I was now my mother's age when I used to think that she was old. I was now stuck in a space where I was complaining about the same things, I once used to hear her complain about. I was thinking the same thoughts she used to share about her mother when she would openly share her opinions, and somehow this moment brought me comfort. Then I wondered if I lived closer to her would I have gotten as close to God? Because when I lived near my mother, and needed to find comfort, I would go to her house, but after I moved, I could no longer run to her for the comfort I was seeking, and realized the only other person that I could run to was God.

Those thoughts fascinated me, so I opened my Bible and headed to the index where I read until I found four verses that seemed to define my truths about what my absence from my parents had brought me over the years. First with my father and then with my mother — I had found that no matter where life took me, there were moments where I had nowhere to run, and nowhere to run to, and that is why the Bible says:

"And I will ask the Father, and He will give you another Helper, to be with you forever, even the Spirit of Truth, whom the world cannot receive, because it neither sees Him nor knows Him. You know Him, for He dwells with you and will be in you. I will not leave you as orphans; I will come to you." John 14:16-18

"God is our refuge and strength, a very present help in trouble." Psalm 46:1

"...teaching them to observe all that I have commanded you. And behold, I am with you always, to the end of the age." Matthew 28:20

"For I, the LORD *your God, hold your right hand; it is I who say to you, 'Fear not, I am the one who helps you.'"* Isaiah 41:13

It will always fascinate me how one moment in my life can change all the other moments yet to come, and this moment taught me that God makes no mistakes when He moves each of us to different places in our lives, because He knows our hearts and knows where we'll search for the answers.

For my mother...

It's not the cup of coffee that I miss; it's all the conversations that we had. You'd say this and I'd say that. How we would talk for hours. Up 'til dawn, just you and me, and once or twice we'd disagree. You'd smile and say, "You love to get your way!" At least that's what I remember. How we could laugh for hours on end, and then we'd start another conversation again. Something so simple I never thought I'd miss. No, it's not the cup of coffee or any of the other. What I miss most of all is being with my mother.

Written for *The Lord's Blessings*

Appointment Thirty-Six

"ONWARD BY FAITH"

"For anyone who calls on the name
of the Lord will be saved."
Romans 10:13

After September 11, my family and I had co-opted a pumpkin patch/corn maze with Kurt and Debbie Chittock on their property in Penn Valley, CA. From May to November, we'd work together to grow a place where our community could come and pick pumpkins and/or simply get lost in the maze, and one day, while I was waiting for a bus load of school kids to arrive, I took a walk.

It was a cool, Wednesday morning in mid-October when I walked out into the middle of our field of pumpkins, bent down on my knees, and began to pray... *"Father, I need You. You know my son, Glenn, and I know that You also see that he's not happy taking the college courses that he's enrolled in. He's trying to find his place in this world, and I don't know how to help him, so if You will, I would like You to guide him. In Jesus' name, amen."* As I finished praying, I heard the first load of school children arriving on their bus, so I brushed off my knees, and I walked onward to greet them.

The morning went quickly, and before I knew it the afternoon had arrived, and I was standing at our snack barn selling all the fun stuff that parents don't want their children to eat, but yet the moment wouldn't be the same without the sweet taste of something filled with sugar, so while I was helping two children decide what they wanted I looked over to the right and out of the corner of my eye I saw my son walking up the dirt road, and toward me. As he approached there was a line of kids, so he walked to the end of the line. I noticed that he didn't look at me until it was it his turn, and I said, *"Hey son. What are you doing here? What did you do today?"*

"I..."

"You what?" I replied.

"Mom, I joined the Marines today."

"YOU WHAT???"

"I joined the Marines today. It was the weirdest thing, because this morning I felt the strongest calling to go and serve my country, so I did it. I joined the Marines."

"But why, Glenn?" I said quietly. *"What would moti-vate you to want to do that?"*

Semper Fi

"Mom, I just know when I woke up this morning, I felt this calling to do it. And, besides you're the one who raised me in Youth and Government and would always tell me the story about the man who carried the flag during the Civil War. You would say, 'Can you believe that during the Civil War someone would carry the American Flag into battle, and before they would ride out the commanding officer would ask, "And, when this flag falls (because it will) who will come and pick it up?"'"

There was nothing else he had to say. He was right. I knew the cost of freedom. Someone's child had been fighting for our freedom every single day of our lives, and now it seemed that my only son wanted to return the favor, so at that moment there was nothing else that I could say.

It was a Tuesday, several months later, when my husband and I were driving Glenn down to Sacramento, where we would drop him off, he would be flown to Miramar for boot camp, and we wouldn't see him again for 13 weeks. I don't think I had ever gone longer than a week his whole life without seeing him, and now I was having to let go of the person I've always known so that he could become the person that God created him to be, but there was a huge fear in me because...

When Glenn was eight years old, we were driving down Hwy 49, when he said to me, *"Mom, one day I'm going to die saving someone."*

"What did you say?" I asked.

"One day I'm going to die saving someone." He repeated.

I didn't know what to say and when I looked over, and saw his face, I knew that there was something about his thought which brought him peace so I said, *"Well, son, that would be a lovely thing to do for someone."* And then I quickly turned my head away from him, and my eyes filled with tears.

While we were driving him to Sacramento, that was all I could think about. Every time I would look over at my son sitting next to me, I would see my eight-year-old boy with a peaceful smile on his face, and within my worry my heart heard, *"Gina. Your son can't die saving anyone. Only My Son can."*

"What?" I silently asked.

"Your son can't die saving anyone. Only My Son can."

Within a moment I knew that the voice I was hearing was from God, so I reached over, grabbed my son's hand, and said, *"You're going to be fine, Glenn. Nothing is going to happen to you."*

"Okay, mom," he replied, with a look of uncertainty as to why I would say that.

"No, you don't understand. You're not going to die serving our country, because you can't die saving someone. Only God's Son can."

"What are you talking about?" he asked.

"When you were eight years old you told me that you were going to die saving someone, and from the moment you joined the Marines I haven't been able to think about anything else, but God just reminded me that you can't save anyone. Only Jesus can."

When my husband and I arrived home from the hardest drive I ever took, the two of us walked into the house, and I immediately grabbed my Bible and sat down at our kitchen table. I then skimmed each page until I found what I was looking for... *"let it be known to all of you and to all the people of Israel that by the name of Jesus Christ of Nazareth, whom you crucified, whom God raised from the dead — by Him this man is standing before you well. This Jesus is the stone that was rejected by you, the builders, which has become the cornerstone.* **And there is salvation in no one else, for there is no other name under Heaven given among men by which we must be saved."** Acts 4: 10-12

I'm blessed to share that four years later my son returned home, and my life was never the same again. It seemed that while he was gone in Iraq serving my country, God sent me on my own journey, and of course I had to write about it. *Onward by Faith: A Mother's Journey to Iraq and Back* was published and purchased by the Marine moms who lived the journey with me, because it's true... Once a Marine Mom. Always a Marine Mom. Semper Fi to my MMO's.

Veteran

To my Gold Star Mothers, I will never forget the sacrifice your child made for my freedom.

To the one who is reading this, please remember the last Sunday in September is "Gold Star Mother's Day," which gives us the opportunity to:

— Honor the children these mothers have lost.

— Share in their sorrow.

— Show our support as they navigate life without the one, they love.

To learn more about Gold Star Mothers of America visit www.goldstarmoms.com.

Appointment Thirty-Seven

"REMEMBER ME!"

"There is no remembrance of former things;
nor will there be any remembrance of later things
yet to be among those who come after."
Ecclesiastes 1:11

It was a Thursday afternoon when I decided that it was time to paint my linen cabinets a shade of green that my mother would have liked, and while I was painting, I was thinking of my grandmother. It seemed that every time I would hold a paint brush my thoughts would immediately go to her so I decided that I would give her a call. It had been a little over two years since my grandfather had passed away and I liked to check on her as often as I could, so I picked up the phone and dialed, *"Hello,"* I heard her say.

"Hey, Nanny. How are you?" I asked.

The two of us started our conversation talking about nothing, but she sounded exceptionally happy, and it was the first time since my grandfather had died where there was something different in her voice, and I had to know what that difference was, so I said, *"You sound wonderful today. It's so nice to have my grandmother back."*

"Oh, Gina. I'm fine, but I'm always a little sad. I am ready to go be with Popo again whenever the good Lord is ready to come and fetch me, but until then I have a

favor to ask of you."

"Yes," I asked.

"Gina, I know that you always talk about writing your grandfather's story. I know how much you loved him, but I was wondering if you would remember me, too and write some things down?"

"Nanny, I would never forget you," I said. *"I love you so much, and of course I will gladly write things down. What do you want me to never forget?"*

Now, I was thinking she would say something like — remember all the Christmases at my house, our fishing and camping trips to Salton Sea or when I'd take you shopping each year for school clothes, etc. But she didn't mention any of those things.

"Remember when you came to my house the year before Popo died and you wrote about what I liked to do. Do you still have that notebook?" she asked.

"Yes, how could I forget that visit? That's when you both invited Jesus into your heart and you bought me that 'I Love Jesus' candle holder that I am looking at as we're speaking. Yes, Nanny. I remember that night. I have it all written down in one of my journals."

"Good. Now grab a piece of paper and a pen and write this down. My mother's name was Mary Bozich, and Bozich means Christmas in Croatian. She was born in Verbose, which means she was born in Croatia. She had two brothers and two sisters. One sister was Aunt Pauline and she lived in San Pedro. My father's name was Ray Mazar, and he died in 1918, eight days after I was born. He was only 26 years old. That was the year of the flu, and you are lucky you never went through anything like that. There was also my sister, Mary, and my brother John. My mother remarried two years later to my stepfather, Mike Muich, and they had two children. My brother Mike, and my sister Dorothy. Did you write all that down?"

"Yes," I replied.

"That's all I need you to remember," she said in a satisfied voice.

The two of us talked for a few minutes more and as we hung up the phone she said, *"Now, don't forget what I told you. Remember what I liked to do, and where*

I came from, okay?"

"*Okay. I promise I will remember. I will talk to you soon. I love you.*"

"*I love you, too.*"

We hung up, and I went back to painting my linen cabinets, and a few hours later, just as I was about to paint my last stroke my phone rang, "*Hello,*" I said.

"*Gina, this is your Aunt Pat. I wanted to call and tell you that as I was driving home from my store this evening, I drove past Nanny's house, and noticed that it was dark and her house lights were not turned on, and all I could see was the reflection of what seemed like the television. So, I pulled into her driveway to check on her. When I entered the house, I found her sitting upright in a chair, and she was unconscious. She had a stroke, and she's at the hospital now. She can't talk, and it looks like you were the last person to talk to her because after she left in the ambulance, I heard a beeping noise and I followed the noise, and it led me to her answering machine. It seems that when you called her, she picked it up, but the machine recorded your whole conversation, and it doesn't seem that anyone called her after you. How did she sound when you called?*"

"*She sounded so good today, but it was odd because she had me write down all the things that she wanted me to remember about her, so I did, and then I told her I loved her and would talk to her soon.*"

"*Okay,*" my aunt said, "*I'm heading to the hospital now. Your mom and I will keep you posted.*"

I hung up the phone in shock, threw away my paint brush, and grabbed my box that was filled with my collection of writing journals, and digging through the box I didn't stop until I found the blue journal. For some reason I remembered that on that visit my blue journal had a rocking horse on it and my grandmother made mention of the horse and when I found it, I opened it, and there I found what I had written...

Tonight I sat down with my grandmother at her kitchen table, and she shared the recipes from her youth. She seemed to love mornings that were warmed by a hot stove in the kitchen, providing smells of sweet cakes rising as if their sole purpose was to awake everyone in the house, *"I used to pull the dough when I was young. When the dough would crack my mother would get terribly mad at me,"* she said.

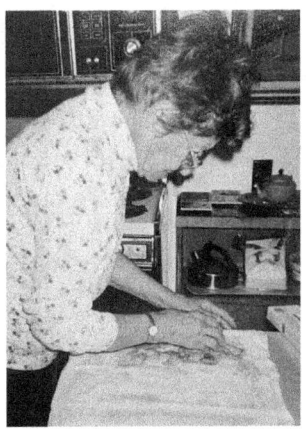

Listening to her tell of her mother and what a wonderful cook she was, was beautiful. She could remember her youth as if she were pulling the dough yesterday. Her eyes would light up as she spoke of her mother's cooking, and she seemed to sit taller as she bragged about her mother's talents.

She and I sat for hours going over recipes, and as she was turning the pages of the cookbooks, she explained to me how she used to love reading them, and their recipes, and how she would tell herself, *"One day I am going to make these dishes."* Most of which she never made. But, when she found her favorite holiday recipes, she would smile and hand me each one, telling me the story of why she loved the comfort she was creating, and showed me the date of the last time she made her wonderful, sweet bread. I sat quietly, listening, and writing down each of her favorite recipes so that I would never forget this night.

We also made homemade strudel, and she walked me step-by-step, as she laid each layer of dough atop another. As she was walking me down her memory lane, I was reminded that each Christmas she would lay out all of her cakes on her buffet table and yell, *"Help yourselves everyone,"* and she would stand by to watch as we each took our first bite.

My favorite memory of her Christmas display was her sweet bread cakes (Kifle) where she would have my grandfather shell the walnuts and she would use them in her cakes. Her sweet bread cakes were beautiful, but deadly, because there were always shells left behind, and if one didn't know to bite softly there was a good chance one would need to see a dentist immediately.

As she was telling me all the stories of her youth, I could see the importance of a mother spending time with their child in the kitchen. Passing down a recipe is so much more than creating a wonderful dish. Mothers are creating life-long memories that will always be sparked by the smell of something wonderful baking in the oven.

I'm so glad I took this time tonight to listen and enjoy the interests of my grandmother. The recipes she shared I will pass down to my children, and I pray that when my children are grown, they won't remember that I didn't cook well, they will remember that well... I cooked!

Then as our night was coming to an end, and my grandmother was heading to bed, she walked over to me and said, *"Here,"* and handing me a piece of paper she continued, *"I want you to keep this and remember it always."*

A Kitchen Prayer

Warm all Thy kitchen with Thy love, and light it with Thy peace.

Forgive me all my worrying and make my grumbling cease.

Thou who didst love to give man food, indoors or by the sea.

Accept this service that I do, I do it unto Thee.

Two weeks later, February 24, 2004.

It was a Tuesday morning when I opened my front door and was heading out to go and visit my grandmother in the hospital, when my phone rang, so I placed my suitcase out on the patio, and returned to answer my phone, *"Hello."*

"Gina, she's gone. She passed away early this morning, going peacefully."

I didn't say a word. I just hung up the phone, and went into my room, laid down on my bed and sobbed, when suddenly, the sunlight came in from my window and shined on a hand-colored photo that I have had since I was a child. The photo was a picture of my grandmother and my Aunt Pat when my aunt was a child. So, I got up, walked over to it, and asked, *"What were you trying to tell me?"*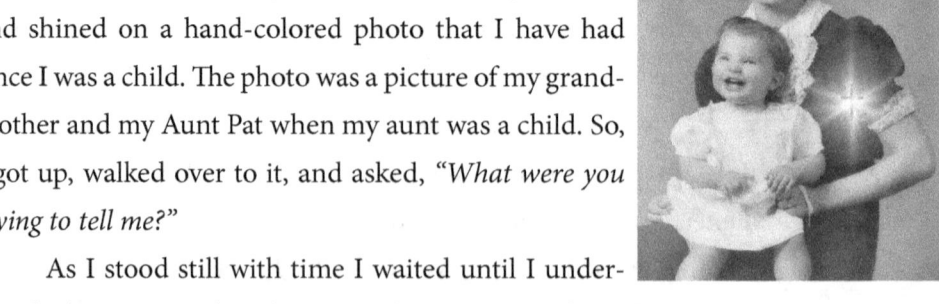

As I stood still with time I waited until I understood what my grandmother wanted me to remember...

Unless things have been written down, recorded, all records of moments will be forgotten, once the last person who remembered is no longer alive. What she was telling me was, *"I won't live long enough to teach your children how to bake my sweet bread cakes or pull dough from the table. Your children never had the opportunity to spend Christmas at my house, and because I was so busy living life, I never got extra moments to teach you all the things that were important to me. So, please remember me when you bake my sweet bread cakes or pull dough from a table. And remember that I too had a family that you never had the opportunity to meet, and once I'm gone, unless you write down their names, and remember them, they too will be gone forever."*

As I stood pondering my peace, I noticed that as the reflection of the sunlight started to disappear, what appeared was the reflection of a tiny cross, and I knew that God was letting me know that she was home. She was fine. And, whenever I missed her all I had to do was bake and there she would be.

For those who love to bake and want to spend a moment with my grandmother.

Sweet Bread Cakes (Kifle)

As told to me by my grandmother

Ingredients:

2 cups sifted flour

1 cup compressed yeast

1 stick butter

2 egg yolks

½ cup dairy cream

Confectioner's sugar

Melted butter

Walnut filling:

1 cup finely chopped walnuts. (Make sure they are shelled!!!)

½ cup sugar

1 tsp. vanilla

2 egg whites, stiffly beaten

Combine walnuts, sugar and vanilla. Fold in stiffly beaten egg whites. Makes enough for two dozen.

Directions: Put sifted flour into a large mixing bowl. Crumble in compressed yeast. Cut butter with a pastry knife until mixture is crumbly. Add egg yolks and dairy cream; mix well. Form into a ball. On a lightly floured board, knead until smooth (five to ten minutes). Divide dough into three equal parts. Wrap in wax paper. Chill in refrigerator for at least one hour. On board sprinkle with confection sugar, roll each part of the dough into a circle. Cut into eight pie shaped wedges. Fill the wide end of each wedge with one teaspoon of walnut filling. Roll up from wide end to point. Place on greased cookie sheets, curving ends to form a crescent shape. Bake in moderate oven (375 degrees) for about 25 minutes, or until golden brown. Dust with confection sugar. Makes two dozen.

Written for *The Lord's Blessings* in loving memory of Katherin Misken
October 23, 1918 – February 24, 2004

Appointment Thirty-Eight

"WHAT DO YOU BELIEVE?"

"Jesus said to her, 'I am the resurrection and the life.
Whoever believes in Me, though he die, yet shall he live,
and everyone who lives and believes in Me shall never die.
Do you believe this?'"

John 11:25-26

In the early 2000s, I penned a column for *The Union* newspaper titled, "Just Mom" and wrote about raising my kids on a small, diversified farm in our historic gold rush community. I also shared stories of the families who lived amongst me.

In December of 2004, I was walking through the supermarket when a young girl approached and asked me a question, but before I could answer her, she was whisked away. For weeks I thought about her question until I decided to use my column for the greater good, and on December 28, 2004, this was published.

Just Mom, by Gina Gippner

I just glanced over at my alarm clock and it was flashing 2:45am. I finally decided it was time to crawl out of bed and answer a question a young girl asked me several weeks ago. Not knowing how to get my answer to her, I've decided to use my column.

Standing in the produce section in Safeway I had this conversation.

"Excuse me, are you Just Mom from the newspaper?"

"*Yes.*"

"*I read one of your stories and you wrote that you pray. Do you believe in Heaven? A few years ago, my parents were in a car accident and killed driving to Idaho. I would like to know if my parents are in Heaven and if you believe there is a God. I'd like to believe that my parents are fine, safe, and happy. I miss them every day, and I can't sleep because I don't know where they are...*"

At that moment a woman came between us and told her not to bother me. I tried to tell her that she wasn't bothering me, but she swept her away before I could say another word. I haven't stopped thinking about that young girl.

So, to the young girl in Safeway, I would like to answer your question.

This past year was extremely hard for me because my son got on a plane to head for Iraq the same morning my grandmother died. My grandmother was like my mother, and I loved her very much. We also sold all our livestock (that I loved dearly,) and we had to put Nellie, our best dog, down. Nellie also happened to be my best friend, and for 15 years she spent every day of her life beside me, and now there's a grave behind my house that reads, "Nellie Gippner, Semper Fi," which means, "Always Faithful." This is just a small example of the trials that life brought me and my family.

Then one Wednesday afternoon, I was driving down Bitney Springs Road. The same road I have been driving for 16 years, and as I was driving, I was doing the same thing as you are. I was looking for an answer to my question which was, "*God, if You're here let me know that You're with me.*"

The moment I said that I turned the corner and there was the answer I was seeking!

If you were to take a ride down Bitney Springs Road in Nevada City, CA you might notice that there's a cross on the side of the road, and it's marked Barry Lee Brooks. Barry was a young boy when he was killed in an auto accident, and because of his mother's efforts, he will never be forgotten, because Barry's mother has tended to his cross since her son's death.

So, how did I find the answer I was seeking?

I realized that Jesus also had a mother and she too tended to His cross, just as Barry's mother tends to his. A thousand years from now, if Barry's family still lives in Nevada County, someone will watch over his cross, reminding those who drive by that while Barry is no longer a resident of this life, he has "crossed" over and is living the rest of his life with God in Heaven — and for me... the cross was God's simple reminder that no matter what roads I travel in life, He is always with me.

So, yes, I believe in God. I believe in Heaven, and I believe that whatever your parents told you about what they believed is what they believed. I'm assuming that they told you about God and Heaven because of your need to know if I believed that, too.

Now, it's your turn to decide what you believe.

To parents who are reading my column — In a few days we will be celebrating the new year. New Year's Eve is a time when we reflect on our past. We stand before mirrors in sadness and step on our scales to see exactly how much weight we need to lose. We plan for our future, and for some reason it brings us hope that things will be different, but truth-be-told, when January 2 arrives, we're right back to where we were December 31.

This year, please do something different, and grab your children and tell them what you believe. If you love Jesus, share that love with them so in the event when something happens to you, your child(ren) will be able to sleep, know and not doubt, smile with hope, and not cry out of fear, because I've seen the face of a child who didn't know what to believe and I'll never forget her. Give your child(ren) the only resolution you can keep this next year, and that is your heart.

A few weeks after my column appeared in the paper, I received an email from the aunt of Barry Lee Brooks. She read my column, and as Paul Harvey used to say, she wanted to tell me the rest of the story, and she wanted me to know that Barry Lee Brooks had an uncle whose name was also Barry Lee, and he was killed in an accident when he was a young man. When Barry's mother gave birth to her son, she named him after her brother. Then after her son, Barry, was killed in Northern California, she went down to Southern California and removed her brother, Barry, from his residence and brought him home to rest next to her son. Now, the two Barry Lees remain side-by-side where she tends to both of their graves.

Appointment Thirty-Nine

"FORGIVEN"

"Let all bitterness and wrath and anger and clamor and slander
be put away from you, along with all malice. Be kind to one another,
tenderhearted, forgiving one another, as God in Christ forgave you."

Ephesians 4:31-32

It was a Sunday afternoon when my phone rang, and on the other end was my husband. I don't exactly remember how the phone conversation started, but I do remember asking him this, *"So, what time are you coming home? I have a ham in the oven and it's almost ready."*

"I'm not." He replied. *"I've moved out!"*

I walked back to his bedroom and then asked, *"What did you take with you?"*

"All that I need."

And that was that. After 20 plus years of marriage, three children, and a lifetime of memories, we hung up the phone, and I was alone with a ham roasting in my oven and no one to eat it with. My son was stationed in San Diego, and my daughters were out for the evening and there I stood in shock pondering what to do next.

Our marriage was not easy. We got married when we were young, and the two of us grew in different ways until we grew apart, and at this point we even had separate bedrooms, but I never saw this coming, because that's how our relationship had always been. From day one, the two of us were inseparable, and then we'd fight, pull apart, and then somehow find our way back to one another. It wasn't perfect by any means, but it was us!

I remember the first day after my husband left is when the shock wore off and worry became my reality. We had been an income of two and now I was an income of one, with bills that had my name written all over them... OH MY GOSH!!! HOW AM I GOING TO SUPPORT US???, my mind yelled in wonder, along with all the million other thoughts that kept me held to my couch, as if a magnet had a hold of my body and wouldn't release me.

Then on Wednesday, three days after my phone call, I was still magnetized to my couch when my phone rang, and I ignored it. It rang again. Then again, and again until I couldn't take it anymore. I got up, walked over to the phone, picked up the phone and slammed the phone down on the receiver, *"TAKE THAT WHOEVER IS CALLING. LEAVE ME ALONE!"* I yelled, hoping that would stop the phone calls.

It didn't.

The phone kept ringing and ringing until finally I picked up the receiver and asked, *"What?"*

"Hello, is this Gina?" an unfamiliar voice asked.

Irritated I answered, *"Yes. Who are you and why are you calling me?"*

"Gina, you, and I have never met before. I am a single mom and live in San Francisco. I contacted you several months back through the commercial on television about you helping families welcome home their soldiers from serving abroad, and well you helped me. You sent a group of people and a marching band to the airport to help me welcome home my son. He's a Marine, and..."

Interrupting her I said, *"I'm so happy your son arrived home and is safe, but I really don't want to talk right now."*

"I know," she said. *"The Lord told me to call you. I know this sounds weird and I don't know if you are a believer, but all morning He put you on my heart, and every time I would call, and you didn't answer, He'd tell me to call again. I am supposed to*

help you with whatever you need."

Immediately I started to sob, until every word I was speaking was unintelligible, and she said, *"Gina, take a deep breath. Take as many as you'd like, and I'll just wait silently until you are ready to speak."*

She must have been on the other end of the phone for at least 20 minutes until I finally said, *"My husband left me, and I don't know what to do. I can't breathe, and I got a new job, but I've called in sick for three days now and if I don't show up tomorrow, my boss told me not to show up at all, and..."*

"Okay, this is what you're going to do," she said. *"I want you to boil some water, and while the water is boiling, I want you to take a shower. Then I want you to put on your favorite pajamas, and then pour yourself a cup of tea and drink it. After you drink your tea, I want you to iron your clothes for tomorrow and then get some rest. And tell your girls to wake you up a few hours before you have to go to work, so you have time to get ready, and then go to your new job. Tomorrow will be a hard day for you, but you won't go alone. God will go with you."*

The woman never did tell me her name, nor did I ask her. I simply thanked her for her phone call, and after we hung up I did exactly what she said, and for the first time in my life I understood why the first thing everyone does when a tragedy arrives is boil water. It's because it gives us something to do when we don't know what to do!

Then... nearly a year later I received a yellow manila envelope with my name written on it. I knew what was inside and knew that it would be appropriate for me to boil some water. While my water was boiling, I opened the envelope and read that after 22 years of marriage my divorce was final, and that was that!

Not knowing what to do I sipped my tea and then I decided I would do the only thing that would bring closer to the day my husband walked out of my life forever, and that was a funeral, so I made a copy of our divorce papers, headed to The Dollar Store and purchase a bouquet of orange lilies, and off to the cemetery I went.

When I arrived, I strolled through the cemetery as if I was looking for an old friend, but what I was looking for was a corner plot where (other than my marriage) no one would ever be buried there, and that is when I found the perfect spot. It was situated 8 feet from the west corner and 10 feet from a woman who had resided there since 1888. I felt confident she wouldn't be disturbed by my ceremony, and since she was buried alone, with no family in sight, I knew my plot would go undisturbed.

Looking around I found a tree branch and using it as my shovel I dug a small hole, and then placed a copy of my divorce papers in the hole, covered it up with dirt and then laid my orange lilies on top, and then reaching into my back pocket I pulled out a piece of paper and read: *Glenn and Gina Gippner got married at the ripe ol' age of 20. They lived in Southern California until their three children (Glenn, Heidi and Shae) were born, and then they relocated to Northern California where they lived until the death of their marriage. The two of them enjoyed spending time with their children, farming, raising livestock, and country music. They are survived by their three children, two dogs, two goats, and a cat. They aged 22 years in marriage.*

Appointment Forty

"IT TURNED OUT SO MUCH BETTER!"

"Trust in the Lord with all your heart, and do not lean on your own understanding. In all your ways acknowledge Him, and He will make straight your paths."

Proverbs 3:5-6

June 7, 2006, was a Wednesday, and I was in my kitchen making coffee for my house filled with guests when my phone rang.

"Mom are the girls home?" my son asked.

"No," I replied. *"Why?"*

"There's been a car accident on Hwy 20 and the radio just reported that two teenagers were killed. Are the girls together?"

"No. They are at work and drove separately." I replied.

We hung up and a moment later my phone rang again, only this time it was my dear friend, Kerri Mullen, *"Gina..."* she said quietly. *"It's the..."*

She didn't need to say another word because her silence said it all, and within a moment I started yelling, *"NO! NO! NO! NOT THE BOYS!"*

"Gina, I'm so sorry..." but before she could say another word my knees buckled, and the weight of my sorrow brought me crashing to the floor. Within a moment I was thinking about the boys. Ryan and Brett were the sons of my best friends, Glenn and Lisa Newman. They also had a daughter, Kate, who was their eldest, and

our families had been best friends from the moment we met 17 years prior. We did everything together from raising our children in 4-H to owning a Goat's Milk Soap business, and now their whole world had just changed and there was nothing that I could do to rewind their clock, and that's when I rewound my clock back eight years, with a memory.

It was my birthday and my ex-husband and Lisa decided that they were going to throw me a surprise party at The Holbrooke Hotel, and to get me there my ex asked me to meet him in the lobby of the restaurant at 7pm so we could have dinner, and that's what I did.

I arrived promptly at 7pm, dressed and ready for a lovely evening when I noticed that no one was waiting for me. I then politely asked the hostess if she had dinner reservations for us at 7pm, and when she replied, *"I'm sorry, but we don't seem to have a reservation for you tonight,"* I became a bit confused. So, I headed down the stairs to use the pay phone and that is when I heard my ex-husband's voice saying, *"Hi, Cathy. This is Glenn, Gina's husband. I'm sorry to be calling you on such notice, but Lisa and I are throwing Gina a surprise party tonight and we had a mix up. You see, this is funny, but I thought Lisa was inviting the guests and Lisa thought I was inviting the guests, so we don't have any guests. We have a DJ, food, some family is here, and if you come, I'll..."*

At that moment I started laughing and when he heard my voice, he turned his head towards me, and smiling he continued... *"and I'll buy you a drink if you can come."*

Then I heard my sister's voice coming down from the stairwell, being followed by a group of people that I had never met before... *"Okay,"* she said, *"today is my sister's birthday and we're throwing her a surprise party, but we forgot to invite her friends, so this is what I want you to do. When she comes in the door yell, 'SURPRISE.' If she looks at you like she doesn't know you then just tell her that you met her at a fundraiser."* Then I heard a guy ask, *"If I'm nice to her can I have some cake?"* My sister yells out, *"ABSOLUTELY!"* and they walked in to where the festivities awaited me.

A few moments later my ex and I walked into the banquet room, where my family, the Newman family, and 15 strangers all yelled, *"HAPPY BIRTHDAY!"*

I loved that moment.

Then about halfway through the evening Ryan came and stood next to me, placing his hands in his pant pockets, and with a somber look he asked, *"Gina, this party didn't turn out like you thought it was going to turn out, did it?"*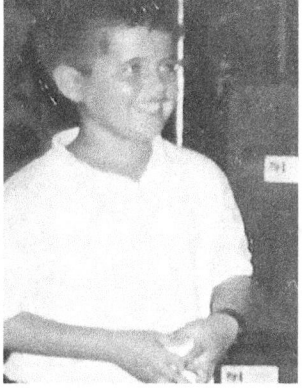

"No, it didn't." I replied.

"I know," he said. *"It turned out so much better!"*

Ryan then ran back to the dance floor and smiled at me, and I knew he was right because all the people I loved were there, and 15 people who I never met, but after that evening, I would never forget them.

"Gina, are you okay?" One of my guests asked, as he lifted me back to my feet. *"You blacked out for a moment. Who was on the phone? Who are the boys?"*

Through my tears I shared that it was Ryan and Brett who were involved in the car accident, and then when my three children arrived home the four of us drove to Lisa and Glenn's home. The moment I walked through their door I saw Lisa through a crowd of people, and without saying a word she made her way to me, we grabbed hands, and she led me into Ryan's bedroom where the two of us fell to our knees and sat within our tears.

A short time after the accident, family, along with a community of friends, gathered on a Saturday at Gateway Western Park in Penn Valley to celebrate the lives of Ryan, 18 and Brett, 15, and in front of the hundreds of people who gathered that afternoon I took a deep breath and retold the story of my surprise party, and when I was done sharing I said, *"The reason I am sharing this story with you today is because I believe with all my heart that when Ryan and Brett entered Heaven Brett looked at Ryan and said, 'Ryan, I bet our car ride didn't turn out like you thought it would, did it?'*

'No, it didn't, Brett!'

'I know. It turned out so much better!'"

"My Father's house has many rooms; if that were not so, would I have told you that I am going there to prepare a place for you? And if I go and prepare a place for you, I will come back and take you to be with Me so that you also may be where I am. You know the way to the place to where I am going." John 14:2-4

In memory of
Brett Matthew Newman
June 4, 1991 – June 7, 2006

In memory of
Ryan Christopher Newman
February 1, 1988 – June 7, 2006

Appointment Forty-One

"GIVE IT TO HIM"

"Blessed rather are those who
hear the word of God and obey it."
Luke 11:28

It was a Sunday afternoon, and I was standing in my kitchen washing dishes, when I happened to look out the window and noticed a beautiful Blue Jay perched on my ol' oak tree. He wasn't doing much of anything other than moving his tiny head from side-to-side as if he was contemplating which way he should fly. I smiled and continued washing my dishes. Then a moment later my heart heard the Lord say, *"Gina, whatever Jay asks you for I want you to give it to him."*

A few moments later my phone rang, and it was Jay calling, and I immediately went and sat down at my kitchen table because I couldn't believe he was calling, *"What's up?"* I asked, *"What do you need?"*

"Oh, I don't know," He replied. *"I was just thinking about you and wanted to call."*

We talked for a moment about nothing and then I asked, *"Jay, is there anything specific for which I can pray? Is there anything that you need?"*

Jay got quiet for a moment and then said, *"Well, if you wouldn't mind praying that God will enable a way for me to go with Twin Cities Church to the Gulf Coast and help rebuild a church that was damaged by Katrina. I would appreciate your prayers."*

"What's holding you back?" I asked.

"$700," he replied.

"Whom do I make the check out to? You or the church?"

"No, Gina. I'm not asking you to pay for it. In fact, I don't even know why I called you. I've never called you before and I know that you recently got divorced, and don't have any extra money. I'm so sorry that I even asked for your prayers, and..."

"Jay, stop talking, please. I was standing in my kitchen, washing dishes, looking at a Blue Jay when the Lord said to me, 'Whatever Jay asks you for I want you to give it to him.' And no sooner did God give me His instructions, you called with a need for $700. Can you believe that out of all the people who know and love you, God asked me to do this for you so you can go and rebuild a church?"

The two of us became silent, because it was almost too much for the two of us to comprehend.

I then asked again, *"Jay, whom do I make the check out to?"*

"Please make it out to the church."

Time passed and when Jay returned from the Gulf Coast we met up for coffee and he told me all about his wonderful trip and the people he met. When our coffee was gone, and it was time to leave Jay looked and me and said, *"Maybe next year I can pay it forward and pay for another person to go on a mission trip."*

But that wasn't God's plans for Jay.

Three weeks after the two of us got together for coffee, Jay found out that he had brain cancer, and for the next two years he ran his race until he crossed his finished line.

On Monday, June 8, 2009, James Maple went home to be with the Lord, and I sat for hours remembering the moment when I was standing in my kitchen, washing dishes, enjoying the Blue Jay and then heard the voice of the Lord telling me to give Jay whatever he needed.

I'm so blessed that I was listening.

Appointment Forty-Two

"DO NOT WORRY"

"Brothers, I do not consider that I have made it my own.
But one thing I do: forgetting what lies behind and
straining forward to what lies ahead."

Philippians 3:13

It was a beautiful Friday morning, when I grabbed my warm cup of coffee, walked over to my front door, and while opening it I said, *"Father God, I have to work to-day and I won't be leaving the house so if You need me to help someone or pass on a message from You, You'll have to send them to me."* I then locked my screen door, walked into my office, and as I went to sit down at my desk, I heard a knock at the screen door.

"HOLD ON. I'LL BE RIGHT THERE!" I yelled, and as I approached the door, I could hear someone crying, *"Melody, is that you? Are you okay?"* I asked.

Melody waited as I hurried to unlock the screen door, *"Please come in. What's wrong?"*

"Oh, Gina. I didn't know where to go. I was driving down Pleasant Valley Road and pulled over at the corner and the Lord told me to come to your house. I wasn't sure which house, but since I was on this corner, I pulled in and to be honest. I'm a little surprised to find you here."

"The Lord told you to come here?" I asked.

GINA MEYER

"*Yes,*" she replied.

"*Melody, you're not going to believe this, but I just opened my front door, and told the Lord that if He wanted me to help someone or pass on a message today, He'd have to send them my way and here you are. What's wrong?*"

"*Oh, Gina. I am getting a divorce and I have nothing. I am so worried about my future, and I don't know what I'm supposed to do.*"

"*Well then,*" I said. "*Here, come and sit down at my kitchen table. I have my Bible right here and let's ask the Lord what you should do.*"

I picked up my Bible, moved it in front of me, and then (while looking at Melody) I said, "*A few weeks ago I was at church and one of the pastors shared that people shouldn't do this, but before he told me I shouldn't do this, I've done this, and God has always answered my question.*"

"*What are you doing?*" Melody asked.

"*I'm going to turn the pages randomly and without looking, and when you're ready I'm going to place my finger on a Bible verse, and I'll do this while looking directly at you. I won't look at the Bible, and wherever my finger lands you must trust that God instructed my heart to place my figure there. Do you trust Him?*" I asked.

"*Yes,*" she replied.

Then without missing a beat I began moving the pages, to-and-fro, and when I could see her concern I said, "*There was a story about a man who wanted to find out what God had for his future, so he closed his eyes, opened the Bible randomly, and stuck his finger on the page. He opened his eyes and read Matthew 27:5, 'Judas... went away and hanged himself.' Not liking that answer, the man tried again. This time his finger landed on Luke 10:37, 'Go and do likewise.' Again, not liking that answer, the man tried again. This time his finger landed on John 13:27, 'What you are about to do, do quickly.'*"

When Melody smiled, I pointed my finger on a verse and said, "*Are you ready to read God's message to you?*"

She smiled, and I began reading... "*Therefore I tell you, do not be anxious about your life, what you will eat or what you will drink, nor about your body, what you will put on. Is not life more than food, and the body more than clothing? Look at the birds of the air: they neither sow nor reap nor gather into barns, and yet your heavenly Father feeds them. Are you not of more value than they? And which of you by being anxious can add a single hour to his span of life? And why are you anxious about clothing? Consider the lilies of the field, how they grow: they neither toil nor spin, yet I tell you, even Solomon in all his glory was not arrayed like one of these. But if God so clothes the grass of the field, which today is alive and tomorrow is thrown into the oven, will He not much more clothe you, O you of little faith? Therefore do not be anxious, saying, 'What shall we eat?' or 'What shall we drink?' or 'What shall we wear?' For the Gentiles seek after all these things, and your heavenly Father knows that you need them all. But seek first the kingdom of God and His righteousness, and all these things will be added to you."* Matthew 6:25-33

Melody could not believe what I had just read to her, and to be honest, neither could I. Out of all the 31,102 verses in the Bible, God had picked the perfect eight, and the moment I saw her smile, I knew that God had sent her to my house so He could deliver His message.

Appointment Forty-Three

"I LOVE PIG STORIES"

"Above all, keep loving one another earnestly, since love covers a multitude of sins. Show hospitality to one another without grumbling. As each has received a gift, use it to serve one another, as good stewards of God's varied grace."

1 Peter 4:8-10

In 2006, New Year's Day was on a Saturday, and I was so excited because on New Year's Eve I had quit my many jobs to start my new life, and when I awoke that morning, I didn't want to get out of bed. I wanted to bask in the fact that after my divorce I had done it. In one year, I had worked many jobs, slept very little, but managed to save enough money that I was able to quit my many jobs and start my own non-profit, and that was the day Owie BowWowie and Friends Foundation was born! (www.iloveowie.org)

New Year's Eve also brought about another change for me. When my son joined the Marines, I joined a group of mothers online, called Marine Moms On-line. It was a chat forum on Yahoo where people would post questions about boot camp or deployments. We'd ask about care packages or what to expect when our children returned home from war. Our questions were endless, but somehow there was always someone who had the answer(s) we were seeking. The group brought me many friends, but it was also where I first decided that I would be brave enough to share my writing, and this is why...

When the War on Iraq broke out on March 20, 2003, mothers were afraid. I can still recall the first post that read: OH MY GOD! THE WAR HAS STARTED!!! WHAT IF MY SON DOESN'T RETURN HOME???

After I read that post, it freaked me out because my son was heading out too, and secondly, I didn't want to read posts that were going to bring me any more stress than I was already under, so I decided that I would write a humorous story about our pig named Daisy, and before I knew it I was (weekly) sharing a tall tale about what it was like raising my children on the farm with the hopes that it would calm the fears of parents. Then, within the next three years, God blessed me with a following of faithful readers who enjoyed reading my stories as much as I enjoyed writing them.

But once my son became a veteran, I decided it was time for me to leave the group, and on New Year's Eve I wrote a post sharing that it was time for me to leave, and I thanked everyone for their friendship.

And, then it happened.

A mother posted... *"Gina, do you have any plans for turning the stories you wrote into a book? I would love to have a copy because your stories got me through my son's deployment."*

I then responded to her post, *"Thank you for your kind words, but no. I have no plans of turning my stories into a book. In fact, my computer broke where I kept all the stories so unfortunately, they are completely lost, and I don't have time to go through the archives but thank you again for your kind words, and I will continue to pray for all those who are serving my country."*

Now this is where I'm going to come back to New Year's morning 2006, where I'm lying in bed not wanting to get out of bed, so I don't. Instead, I grab my computer, open my email, and see that I have over 400 emails in my inbox, and confused by the influx I open one and read, *"Gina, I read that you lost all your stories. Here are four of my favorites. I hope this helps and you can find the rest and publish your book."*

Then I opened another email, and it was the same thing. Email after email people were sending me back my stories until I realized that every one of my stories were emailed back to me because people kept them, and I was blown away by their kindness.

As I was getting ready to close my computer, I decided I would open one last email before I got out of bed and the email read, *"Hi Gina. We don't know each other personally, but I LOVE PIG STORIES, and if you need help putting your book together, please give me a call @ …-…-… and I will help you."* Jan Moon

Without thinking I picked up my phone and dialed her number, and from the moment we said, "hello" we became the best of friends. We talked for hours, and it wasn't until I realized how late it was, I said, *"Hey, Jan. What are you doing next week?"*

"Nothing, why?" she asked.

"I just quit my many jobs and I'm heading down to San Diego next week to meet with my toy manufacturer for my non-profit I'm starting, and I know that your son is stationed in San Diego. It seems that God has put it on my heart to ask you, if you'd like, I will fly you to Sacramento, and you can go with me, and we can visit your son. It won't cost you anything, but your time. And then maybe we could work together and publish a book with all the stories that everyone just sent me. What do you think?"

Jan didn't say a word. She lived in Louisiana, and was probably thinking, well, I just met this woman over the phone, but then she said, *"Can I call you back? I want to pray about it and ask my mama."*

I loved that she wanted to pray about my offer and ask her mama, and that's exactly what she did. A few hours later she called me back, accepted my offer and a few days later I drove to the Sacramento Airport, and it wasn't until I saw a woman coming down the escalator, wearing a sign that read I LOVE PIG STORIES, did I recognize her.

The two of us hugged and I drove us to my house. When we returned home, I was exhausted. I still hadn't caught up on my past year of sleep so I asked, *"Jan, I'm*

so sorry, but would you mind if I rested for about an hour? I hate to leave you like this, but I just haven't been able to catch up on my sleep."

She immediately gave me a hug and said, *"You get some rest."* And I rested.

About an hour or so later I awoke to this sweet smell of nothing I had ever smelled before and I followed the smell into my kitchen, and that is where I found Jan. She was standing next to my stove, wearing my apron, stirring a pot of Heaven, and when she saw me, she asked, *"Are you hungry?"*

I immediately walked over to my breakfast bar, sat down and immediately started to cry, *"What's wrong?"* Jan asked.

"This year has been such a hard year, and when I came out and saw you cooking in my kitchen it was overwhelming. I imagine this is what Jesus means when He says, 'As each has received a gift, use it to serve one another, as good stewards of God's varied grace.'"

Jan walked over to where I was, gave me a hug, and without saying another word she served me up a bowl of gumbo and her homemade biscuits. It was a moment that I knew I would treasure forever.

The following week the two of us took a road trip to San Diego that was nothing like Thelma and Louise's adventure, but just as memorable.

Jan and I went on to work together, and in 2007 we published *Onward By Faith: A Mother's Journey to Iraq and Back*, and to this day we have remained the best of friends. I often wonder what my life would have been like if I didn't listen to God and invite Jan to fly from

*In memory of
Jan Moon
August 24, 1953 –
June 28, 2024*

Louisiana to California, and drive from Northern California to Southern California and back again. because I do believe I would have missed one of the greatest friendships of my life, and I never would have experienced God's grace coming from her kindness in my kitchen.

Appointment Forty-Four

"TIME TO FORGET!"

"Brothers, I do not consider that I have made it my own. But one thing I do:
forgetting what lies behind and straining forward to what lies ahead,
I press on toward the goal for the prize of the upward call of God in Christ Jesus.
Let those of us who are mature think this way, and if in anything you think otherwise,
God will reveal that also to you. Only let us hold true to what we have attained."

Philippians 3:13-16

It was a Wednesday evening, and I was packing up my house to move. Since my divorce, the past few years had been difficult, and when I started working from home, my home became very quiet. My son was living in San Diego, and my girls had moved down to southern California. So I decided I could use a change too, and where better to be than near my children.

As I was packing, I opened a drawer and found something that was wrapped in aluminum foil, and feeling like Nancy Drew I had to unwrap the foil to uncover the mystery that awaited me. Therefore, I immediately went and sat on my bed and slowly opened it. To my surprise I had found a pink can-dle that I had forgotten about. It was my birthday candle that was numbered from 1 to 21 from top to bottom, and each year I would burn it down until I arrived at the age that I was celebrating. Also attached to the candle was

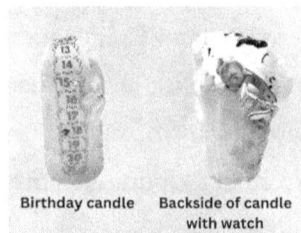

Birthday candle   Backside of candle
with watch

my Cinderella watch... the same watch that my father had given me the last time I had seen him. And then I remembered...

On my 12th birthday, the day my father drove away, I came into my house and burned the candle down to number 12. I then placed it on the shelf with my watch beside it. Both seemed to represent time, and I promised myself that I would never burn the candle down until I spent another birthday with my father.

I never did.

With time, the years passed, and before I knew it, I was over 21, and since my watch no longer fit my wrist, I placed the watch on top of the candle and wrapped them in foil, and that was that. The two items had been sitting in my drawer for decades, only to be forgotten, and that's when I decided it was time to let go of any hope of ever finding my father again, so I threw the watch in the trash and rewrapped the candle back in the foil and placed it in a box.

"*Hello! Is anyone home?*"

"*Melody, is that you?*" I yelled.

"*Yes, I've been knocking but you didn't hear me at the front door. What are you doing?*"

"*Well, I am just packing up and you're not going to believe this, but I found my ol' Cinderella watch that my father gave me the day he drove off, and my birthday candle. I decided that today I would throw away the watch, but for whatever reason I've decided to pack up the candle.*"

Melody looked at me with such sadness and said, "*Gina. No. You can't throw away that watch because if you do you will never get it back.*"

"*I don't want to get it back. I've kept that watch for decades hoping that one day my father would find me, and he never did, and it's time that I let go of this silly dream. I believe I've kept it long enough because, well... it is a Cinderella watch, and we both know the song she sings about a dream is a wish your heart makes. I am tired of this dream because it breaks my heart when I think about it and I'm finally letting it go... Actually, I've got an idea.*"

At that moment, I reached into my trash can, picked up the watch and said,

"Follow me, Melody. I'm going to dispose of this correctly."

Melody followed me out my front door, down my graveled driveway, and as I opened the gate Melody gasped, *"Oh no, Gina. You're going to throw your watch in that are you? When they pick up your trash in the morning you will never be able to get it back. Are you sure you want to do this?"*

"I'm sure," I said, and then threw the watch into the trash bin. When I heard the watch hit the bottom of the can I closed the lid, walked away, and never looked back.

That night I decided that I would sleep with my bedroom window open so that I would be able to hear when the trashman came to pick up my trash, but for some reason I couldn't sleep so I grabbed my ol' rocking chair, placed it by my bedroom window and the whole night I waited and rocked. Then I heard it. The sound of the roar turning onto my street, then I saw the headlights as they followed until the screech of the brakes stopped in front of my house and the man jumped out.

The moment the man jumped out of his garbage truck I wanted to run down my driveway and yell, *"STOP! WAIT!"* But I didn't. I watched as he picked up my trash can, threw it in the back, placed my trash can back to where he had collected it from and drove away.

And that was that. For the first time I completely understood why I had to throw my watch away!

It was the only piece of evidence that proved I had a father, but it wasn't my father. It was a memory of my father driving away that I seemed to think about every time I saw the watch, and for the first time I realized it was time to forget what lay behind me and move onward to what lies ahead.

Appointment Forty-Five

"TILL DEATH WILL WE PART"

"Do everything in love."

1 Corinthians 16:14

It was a hot Saturday in July, the 4th to be exact, when Kenny Woods wandered back into my life. Kenny and I were friends in high school, and after we reconnected, we dated for a little over a year, until one Saturday in October we decided that we would get married, and that's what we did.

We married.

Our wedding ceremony took place within Kenny's beautiful garden, where we were surrounded by family, numerous friends, and goldfish that swam upon each tabletop to our wedding theme of "The Perfect Catch." And of course, others had to get in on the fun and toast us while saying things like...

"Let's toast to two less fish in the sea!"

"Out of all the fishes in the sea, these two were meant to be!"

"I'm so glad she's hooked on you, because you'd be left with nothing more than your dirty shoes!"

During the evening the toasts became too silly to

When Gina Gippner became Gina Woods

remember, but the one thing that I'll never forget was the one question that many people seemed to ask me, *"So, Gina. How is this going to work between the two of you?"*

The first time I was asked the question I replied, *"What are you talking about?"*

"You know. The faith difference," my guest replied. *"You know. You are a Christian, and a strong one. Kenny is an atheist, and a strong one. How is this supposed to work between you two, and besides, doesn't the Bible say you're not to be unequally yoked?"*

By the end of our wedding reception, I was so tired of answering the same question over and over again that I snapped at my last guest as she was leaving and said, *"Yes, it says that, but who am I to judge if Kenny is a Christian or not? He's a nice person and he treats me well."*

"If your whole life wasn't built on you wanting to personally know God I wouldn't have said a thing," she replied. *"So, we will just have to wait and see how this works out for the two of you, because the two of you will always be at odds with each other unless one of you crosses over to the other side of the bridge. I don't see you ever doing that, and I don't see Kenny ever doing that, so we shall see who is right... God when He says, 'Do not be unequally yoked with unbelievers'... or you."*

"Yes, we shall see," I said in a near whisper.

After all our guests had gone home, and our house was quiet I asked Kenny this, *"Hey, do you think you're ever going to want to know more about God?"*

"NO," he said abruptly.

"But, what if you're wrong?" I asked. *"The Bible says that everyone who believes may have eternal life in him. For God so loved the world that He gave His one and only Son, that whoever believes in Him shall not perish but have ever lasting life. For God did not send His Son into the world to condemn the world, but to save the world through Him. So, whoever believes in Him is not condemned but whoever does not believe stands condemned already because they have not believed in the name of God's one and only Son."*

"Well, I guess we'll do what we said in our wedding vows," he replied.

"What's that?" I asked.

"Till death will we part."

Truer words were never spoken.

Appointment Forty-Six

"BORN FOR SUCH A TIME AS THIS"

"And it shall come to pass afterward, that I will pour out my Spirit on all flesh; your sons and your daughters shall prophesy, (the foretelling or prediction of what is to come) your old men shall dream dreams, and your young men shall see visions."

Acts 2:17

It was a Tuesday morning when I awoke from a prophetic dream that shared with me that I was going to be a grandmother. I could see Jesus holding the child, I just couldn't tell if it was a boy or a girl. And I didn't know which child of mine was going to bring me the news.

A few hours later (as I was busy working in my office) an email appeared from an unknown address. I almost didn't open it but then something prompted my heart to, and when I did, the caption simply read:
THIS IS FOR YOU!

I couldn't believe my eyes because what was sent to me was a drawing of Jesus holding a child and I knew that was for me, so I printed it out, taped it onto my whiteboard and got back to work.

About an hour later I heard a knock at the front door, and I yelled, *"Come in,"* and in walked my son and Heather, and I knew.

"*Mom, Heather and I have something to tell you.*"

"*That you're going to have a baby!*" I replied.

My son just smiled, because he knew how I knew, but Heather didn't, "*How did you know?*" she asked.

"*I had a dream last night with Jesus showing me a baby.*" At that moment, I pointed to the drawing on my whiteboard and continued... "*I received an email today with this drawing. I just couldn't tell if it's a boy or a girl, and I didn't know what child of mine was going to bring me the news, but I knew the good news would arrive.*"

"*Why would God give you a dream?*" Heather inquisitively asked.

"*In the Bible God gave many people dreams and visions, and I can only be a witness to how God has chosen to communicate with me. It's interesting because many people don't believe God still gives us visions and dreams today, but God says, 'I change not' so why would He change His mind and not talk to me through a vision or a dream? He talks when He wants to talk, and I trust my dreams, and His voice when I hear Him. I will never allow any person to tell me the only way He speaks to us is through His written Word, because I can't always carry a Bible around with me. I can, however, trust the knowledge that He tells me because I know His voice.*"

"*And... being that you are carrying my first grandchild, of course, God would want to be the first one to personally remind me that... Every child conceived; He gave His consent.*"

It was a Monday morning, seven months later, when I had placed my cup of coffee on my office desk and as I was reaching to turn my computer on my phone rang... "Hello!"

"*Mom, if you hurry to the hospital you should arrive on time to witness the birth of your granddaughter.*"

I hung up the phone and quickly drove to the hospital and the moment I saw her come into the world I knew that... "*she was born for such a time as this.*" Esther 4:14

Appointment Forty-Seven

"HASTA LA VISTA, BABY"

*"The L*ord* has made everything for its purpose."*
Proverbs 16:4

It was a Tuesday afternoon in July when I was sitting in my office, working, drinking tea, and watching the curtains blow towards me from the summer wind. I could smell the fragrance of our orange tree that was ripe for its scent. My afternoon was perfectly delightful, and I thought to myself, it would take a bomb to go off to ruin this day.

A moment later I noticed that my mail had fallen to the floor from the wind, so I picked them up and decided that there was no better time to go through my bills, and one by one I opened each of them until I got to a letter that was written from my insurance company:

"Gina Woods,

We regret to inform you that because you neglected to pay the increase of $30.00 in June, your insurance has been cancelled. To reinstate your policy, you will need to give our office a call at..." R-YOU-KID-DING. I was so angry!

I immediately called my insurance agent, and she told me that because of my age my policy had gone up by $30.00 a month, and because I didn't pay it, they cancelled me.

"But they automatically take the money out of my bank account." I said. *"It's*

an automatic withdrawal. Why didn't they just take out the money? They took out the original cost of what they've been charging me every month. Is there anything you can do?"

Unfortunately, there was nothing she could do to help me get my old policy reinstated without it costing me a small fortune, but before our phone call ended, I was back to being insured. After I hung up the phone, I grabbed a piece of paper and wrote $485 \times 36 = 17,460$. That's how much I had spent on health insurance over the past three years, and I never once went to the doctor, so I picked up the phone and made an appointment, because I had decided that never again would I spend that much money and never use a penny of it!

A week later, on a Thursday, I walked into Dr. Toomer's office, and the two of us chatted. He asked me how my kids were doing because he had delivered all three of them. He wondered where I had been, because it seemed to him that I had forgotten that I had ovarian cancer in my early 30's and was supposed to be seen at least once a year, *"Where have you been, Gina? It's been a while?"* he asked.

"Oh, I've just been busy working and enjoying family," I replied.

While he was examining me, we continued with small talk until his eyes grew worried and he said, *"Okay. I need you to get dressed and head over to the hospital. We need to get an ultrasound done today."* Neither one of us said another word, he handed me a slip of paper and off I went.

When I arrived at the hospital, they directed me towards where I needed to go and when I was done the radiologist came out and said, *"Gina, I spoke to your doctor, and he needs you to come back to his office right now."*

When I arrived back at Dr. Toomer's office, he sat me down and started to talk, and this is what I heard him say, *"Gina, you have a large ovarian tumor that needs to be removed as soon as possible because if we don't remove it, by the end of this year you won't be here. Now, I need you to go straight to the oncologist. He's the best and I was hoping he would see you today. He's agreed to see you, but you need to be there in 10 minutes."*

I had no time to ask him any more questions, I just had to find my way to the oncologist within 10 minutes, and then I found myself sitting in the oncologists office while he talked, and this is what I heard him say, *"Gina, you have a large ovarian tumor that needs to be removed as soon as possible because if we don't remove it, by the end of this year you won't be here."*

I thanked him for his service, and quickly walked out of his office, and while I was walking through the parking lot to my car, I thought about a scene from the movie Kindergarten Cop, where Det. John Kimble, played by Arnold Schwarzenegger, is frustrated and talking to his class filled with kindergarteners, and a little boy asks him if he's alright and he says, *"I just have a little headache,"* and then another child responds, *"Maybe it's a tumor,"* and frustrated, Det. Kimble, says in his accent, *"IT'S NOT A TOO-MAH! It's not a too-mah."*

And, without thinking I stopped in the middle of the parking lot and yelled, *"IT'S NOT A TOO-MAH!"* Got in my car and drove away.

As I was driving home, and my stress seemed to calm itself, I pulled my car over, called the oncologist, scheduled another appointment with him, and for the next month I spent my time doing one test after another only to find out that both doctors were right... If I didn't have the surgery to save my life, I would have no life left. So on a Wednesday afternoon my two doctors joined their surgical hands together to remove my tumor, and before they put me under, Dr. Toomer asked, *"Do you have anything you want to say before we put you to sleep?"*

"Yes," I said. *"When you both told me I had a tumor I had to find some humor in dealing with this so without going into a long-drawn-out story about why I did this,... I named my tumor 'Arnie,' after Arnold Schwarzenegger, and I would appreciate it very much if when you remove the tumor you say, 'Hasta la vista, baby.'"*

They laughed, and off to sleep I went. When I arrived home, I went into my office and there, on top of my pile of mail lay the insurance bill, and I knew. I knew that God had orchestrated my insurance to be cancelled over a measly $30.00 because had I let another year go by that might have been the end of my story.

But it wasn't.

Appointment Forty-Eight

"THE FUR-REAL STORY OF LOVE"

"Shout for joy, you heavens; rejoice, you earth; burst into song,
you mountains! For the LORD comforts His people and will
have compassion on His afflicted ones."

Isaiah 49:13

If you were to ask me about my mother's gift, it would undoubtedly be sewing. She was like Cinderella's fairy godmother, transforming inexpensive fabric into ballroom-worthy gowns, albeit without the wand. I remember one Saturday in high school, walking into her sewing room to find her crafting a charming little yellow dog pillow. Its head was cocked to one side, prompting me to ask, *"Did the dog get hurt? Is that why its head is tilted?"* She replied, *"No, Gina. I haven't finished sewing it yet. It will look different when I'm done."* Laughing, I said, *"Well, it looks like it has an owie now, so I'm going to name him Owie BowWowie."* In that moment, my heart sparked with a sense of purpose, a divine calling to create an Owie BowWowie. I didn't know why or for whom, but I knew someday it would happen.

Years passed, I moved out, got married, had children, but the desire in my heart to create Owie BowWowie never went away. I talked about "Owie" all the time, but I still didn't know why I would need to make one or for whom.

Then in my early thirties, I was hospitalized for a serious illness, and due to the lack of beds in the adult ward, they placed me in the pediatric ward, where my little roommate was recovering from surgery due to a brain tumor.

For three days I watched as no one came to visit her, and on the third day I called the nurse over to my side of the room and asked, *"What's her story? I have three children, and I would never leave my child in the hospital alone."*

"Gina, she doesn't have any family," she quietly said, and then turned away and walked out of our room.

The following day the nurse brought the little girl a stuffed dog, and as soon as the nurse walked out the door, I saw the stuffed dog go flying across the room until it smacked into the wall, so I got out of bed, retrieved the stuffed dog, and brought it back to the little girl and asked, *"Honey, what's wrong? Why did you throw the stuffed dog across the room?"*

"THAT'S NOT MY TOY... IT'S BROKEN."

At that moment I noticed that the stuffed dog's ear was ripped, and thinking quickly I noticed gauze that was lying on the table next to her bed, so I picked up the gauze, bandaged its head to match the little girls, and handing the stuffed dog back to her I said, *"Honey, it's not broken. He has an owie like you. He's your Owie BowWowie."*

And that was the moment Owie BowWowie was born.

Within a flash of placing Owie BowWowie in the little girl's arms I knew exactly why there was no room for me in the adult ward of the hospital, and why God placed me in the room with the little girl — He needed me to give her comfort... because the Lord comforts His people and has compassion on His afflicted ones.

I couldn't get over how far back God placed this desire within my heart, or how I thought about Owie BowWowie daily, always wondering why I would need to make one and for whom... but when it was time to deliver His message, a gift of comfort, a moment of compassion to one of His afflicted ones, He knew that I would know what to do, and I would do it!

After I left the hospital, I couldn't stop thinking about the little girl, and the importance of giving comfort to hospitalized children, and it was on my ride home where God reminded me that there are hundreds of thousands of children each year who should be given a gift of comfort while they're undergoing their medical treatment, and that is when I decided that I would spend the rest of my life giving comfort to hospitalized or hurt children one Owie at a time. I just had to figure out how to do that.

Then twelve years later the vision of comfort finally became a reality and Owie BowWowie was an adorable stuffed, plush dog, who came with his own bandages, storybook, website, and was created specifically for hospitalized and hurt children. He was perfect.

Then on a Friday, in February of 2012, I put out a request on Facebook asking my friends if they knew anyone who knew anything about starting a non-profit, and that is when my friend, Richard Norris, introduced me to his friend, Kelly Barker.

Shortly after our introduction Kelly and I became instant friends, and because Kelly lived in Michigan, and I lived in Southern California I mailed her an Owie BowWowie so she could personally see him. When he arrived at Kelly's business her brother, Russ Barker, happened to see Owie BowWowie on her desk and asked, *"If Owie BowWowie is all heart, why doesn't he have one?"*

Kelly immediately called and asked me the same question and then she said, *"Would you mind adding a heart to Owie BowWowie's chest?"*

"Of course," I said. *"What a brilliant idea! He needs one."*

February 7, 2012, was a Tuesday, three days after Russ shared that Owie Bow-Wowie needed a heart, that I was sitting in my office sewing a heart on Owie Bow-Wowie, when Kelly called and told me that her brother had gone snowmobiling that morning and died in an accident.

And that was the moment when Owie BowWowie's heart began to beat and continues to beat in remembrance of Russ Barker.

Today, Owie BowWowie's mission is to bring comfort and joy to the 500,000 children in the U.S. facing life-threatening conditions, one Owie at a time. To learn more, visit iloveowie.org, or share about a non-profit close to your heart at gina@iloveowie.org. I'd love to hear how you're spreading comfort to others.

APPOINTMENT FORTY-NINE

"TO GIVE OR NOT TO GIVE: THAT IS THE QUESTION"

"Bring the full tithe into the storehouse, that there may be food in My house. And thereby put Me to the test," says the LORD of hosts, "if I will not open the windows of Heaven for you and pour down for you a blessing until there is no more need."
Malachi 3:10

It was a Sunday morning in June, and I was heading out the door to church when Kenny called out, *"Whatever you do today, please don't tithe! I respect your faith, but please don't give any of our money away."* I didn't respond, but as I drove, I heard a gentle whisper in my heart, *"Give everything in your wallet."* My mind raced, *"Wait, didn't my husband just say the opposite?"* I asked God for a sign, *"If this is really You, have the pastor preach on tithing, and I'll know it's not just me thinking... no one is going to tell me what to do!"*

When I arrived at church, I found my seat, sang with the choir from the pew, and from the moment the pastor asked us to *"Please be seated,"* he preached on giving and he didn't stop until the offering plate was passed around. With a sense of peace, I reached into my purse and gave all I had — $80. That evening, Kenny asked if I had given money to the church, and I hesitated, but finally confessed, *"Yes, I did."* He was surprised, *"But I asked you not to!"* I smiled, *"God asked me to, and in this instance, I had to listen to God."*

The following Wednesday I opened our mailbox to find an unexpected envelope addressed to me. As I tore it open, my heart raced with excitement. Inside was a check for $880 from a company that had purchased a toy I had created — a surprise windfall! I ran to share the news with Kenny, *"I told you God asked me to tithe!"* In that moment, I learned a valuable lesson: I could never outgive God. His generosity and faithfulness far surpass me every time.

Appointment Fifty

"34 YEARS LATER"

*"There is a time for everything, and a season for
every activity under the heavens."*
Ecclesiastes 3:1

It was Tuesday, October 14, 2010, when I was sitting at my computer, working on this book, chatting with Melody on the phone when suddenly an ad popped up from PeopleFinders asking me if I knew Herman Kaleve. Without thinking, I asked Melody, *"Hey, do you know anyone named Herman Kaleve?"* *"No,"* she said. *"Well, I do,"* I replied. *"That's my biological father's stepdad."* *"Well, is there a phone number?"* she asked. *"I don't know."* *"Well, look. Hit the link and see if anything pops up."*

It took me a few minutes to do it, but when I finally mustered enough courage to hit the button, sure enough, there was a phone number. It took Melody another hour to convince me to hang up the phone with her and call Herman to see if he knew what happened to my father. When the phone began to ring, I couldn't breathe because it had been 34 years since I had last seen him, and just as I was about to hang up the phone, I heard, *"Hello."*

"Hello, who is this?" I asked.

"Wait a minute. You called me. Who is this?"

"My name is Lisa. Who is this?" I asked. For some reason, I didn't want to share my real name with the voice on the other end of the phone.

"My name is Richard. Who is this? Who is this really?" he asked. For a moment, I didn't say a word, and then silently I answered, *"Gina. My name is Gina."*

"I have a daughter named Gina. Please tell me this is my daughter."

"I'm your daughter."

The two of us didn't say a word. We simply sat in silence for what seemed like minutes, and it wasn't until he asked me if I had ever gotten married and had kids that our conversation began and continued for hours. I never asked him where he had been for the past 34 years because there was no point. Thirty-four years had passed, and now it was up to us to see where we would take the years we had left. When we hung up the phone, I sat in silence, realizing that he was the person I had remembered from my past. He had the same voice, laugh, and within a moment of panic, I ran to my closet to open up the box that I kept my Cinderella watch in that he had given me for my 12th birthday, and remembered that Melody was right. I never should have thrown the watch away because it was now gone forever.

A year-and-a-half later, 2012.

It was a Wednesday, and I was helping Kenny clean the garage when I said to him, *"You know, I'm not sure if I want to personally see my father. We talk on the phone every now and again, but we never talk about what happened, and at this point, I'm not sure I'll ever find out the truth, because there are always two sides to every relationship, and I will never know which of my parents is telling the truth."*

Then right when I finished my sentence my phone began to ring, and on the other end was Judy MacDonald, the only girlfriend that I remembered from when I was a child. She called to tell me that (while she and my father were no longer dating) they had remained good friends, and he had given her a copy of my book, *Onward by Faith: A Mother's Journey to Iraq and Back.* When she had finished reading it, the Lord put it in her heart to call and tell me the truth about my father.

I nearly dropped the phone. I couldn't believe that no sooner had I said, *"I'm not sure I'll ever find out the truth,"* she was calling to share her truth. *"Well, what's the truth? He left me, and I can't find any reason for a parent to leave a child. I have three children, a granddaughter, and just watch someone try to keep any of them away from me."*

The phone got quiet, and then she lowered her voice and said, *"Gina, you need to go and see him. You need to know the truth, and since I've read your book, you need to see how much alike the two of you are. You will regret not seeing him. Please take a drive."*

"And that's another thing," I said. *"It's been over a year since I first spoke with him, and why hasn't he gotten in his car to come and see me? If I found my child, I would have taken a plane, train, automobile, bike, horse, pick one."*

"Gina, he doesn't drive. He hasn't left his home in years. Just do you both a favor and go and see him. I know that you are hurt, but you are your father's daughter. I don't know what else to say other than God put it in my heart to call you. Do with it what you will."

We hung up the phone, and I didn't say a word. I continued cleaning the garage until I came to a box that I had neglected to mark when I had moved. Being that I was on a quest to know every truth presented to me that day, I had to see what was inside. To my surprise, there was nothing of value until I came to an object wrapped in aluminum foil. For the life of me, I couldn't remember what it was, so I unwrapped it. Inside was my birthday candle that I had burned for my 12th birthday, promising myself that I would never burn it again until I saw my father. But as I was turning it right-side up, I heard something fall to the floor. When I looked down, I couldn't breathe.

"Are you alright?" Kenny asked.

"No. Look what I found."

"Yeah, it's an old kid's watch. So?"

"You don't understand. This is the Cinderella watch that my dad gave me for my 12th birthday. I threw this watch away in the trash when I was packing up to move. Melody and I put it in the trash bin. I stayed up all night and watched as the trashman drove it away. How is it here? I can't believe that it's back from where I last kept it, and to find it today." When I finally caught my breath, I bent down, picked up the watch, and time stood still, literally, because the time on the broken watch read 10:14, and

the date when I reconnected with my father on the phone was October 14.

"*Gina, are you okay?*" Kenny asked.

"*I don't know. I was just remembering back to the last time I saw my dad. I was 12, and as I was getting out of his car, he reached into his glove compartment and pulled out a small box that was covered in black velvet. He handed me the box and said, 'It's funny that you would ask me today if I believed in God, because there is an appointed time for everything.' He then leaned over and hugged me. A hug that lasted only a moment, but the scent of his cologne stayed with me for decades. As he drove away, I stood out in my driveway and watched. When I could no longer see his taillights, I opened the box and found this Cinderella watch. My father was right when he told me, 'There is an appointed time for everything!'*"

A week later, my daughter Shae and I got into the car and drove down to meet my father. When we arrived, I knocked on the door, and as it swung open, I almost took a step backward. The man I had last seen was 36 years old, but the man before me now stood at 70. Despite the years, he retained the same smile, voice, and laughter. He welcomed us inside, and immediately I felt a sense of familiarity. Books lined the shelves, CDs with names both familiar and foreign scattered about. Catching my gaze, he said, "*Please, have a seat. I'd like to play something for you. See if you remember this.*"

I heard...

"*While I was walking down the beach one bright and sunny day I saw a great big wooden box a-floatin' in the bay I pulled it in and opened it up and much to my surprise Ooh, I discovered a boom-boom-boom, right before my eyes...*"

"*I picked it up and ran to town as happy as a king, I took it to a guy I knew who'd buy most anything. But this is what he hollered at me as I walked in his shop 'Ooh, get outta here with that boom-boom-boom before I call the cop. Ooh, get outta here with that boom-boom-boom before I call a cop.*"

The song played until it arrived at its outro...

"*The moral of this story is if you're out on the beach and you should see a great big box, and it's within your reach, don't ever stop and open it up. That's my advice to you. Cause you'll never get rid of the boom-boom-boom, no matter what you do. Oh, you'll never get rid of the boom-boom-boom, no matter what you do."*

He played "The Thing" sung by Phil Harris, a song we used to sing together in the car during our visits.

"Gina, do you remember this song?" he asked.

It took every ounce of strength not to cry in that moment because I didn't remember the words or its singer, but I remembered driving with him as a child singing a song that went something like, *"You better get out with thump, thump, thump, and don't come back no more..."* and as we would sing we would hit our hands on the dashboard of his car, *"thump, thump, thump."* When we'd get to the last "thump" in the song my father would reach over, grab me, and I would scream in the excitement of the moment. At that moment I realized the thump, thump, thump, was actually the boom-boom-boom, and the song was right... I never got rid of the boom-boom-boom no matter how hard I tried, because memories are a hard thing to erase.

Appointment Fifty-One

"GOD USES THE ORDINARY
TO DO THE EXTRAORDINARY"

"Do not neglect to do good and to share what you have,

for such sacrifices are pleasing to God."

Hebrews 13:6

It was a Sunday morning in May when I was driving down Interstate 5, heading back home to Northern California. After years of marriage, Kenny and I decided that there was much truth to the Christian and the atheist not being married. It wasn't that I was "just" a Christian and he was "just" an atheist. We were both very strong in our belief and when two people were as passionate as we were, it wasn't easy for either one of us. With mutual respect and kindness, we decided to amicably part ways in marriage, so we divorced and continued onward with our lives in friendship.

As I drove, my cell phone rang, and Melody's warm voice filled the line. *"Gina, don't lose faith in love,"* she encouraged. *"You've endured a husband who left and another who never truly understood you, but you're still young enough to enjoy the rest of your life with someone that you can simply be you with, and where you can pursue the passions God has placed in your heart — share Jesus, finish your book, Appointments with God, that you've been working on since you were 12! I hope you complete it someday. Most of all, I want to see you happy."*

"I don't ever want to get married again, Mel. My kids are grown, and all I want to do is get my house back, open my store for Owie BowWowie, and spend time with my grandchildren and grow old in peace. Is that too much to ask?"

"That's nuts, Gina. At least be open to the idea of finishing your life well."

"Okay, Mel, this is what I'm going to do. I'm going to ask God this. 'God, if You want me to be with someone you have 30 days to bring him to me. And, he must be my "Notebook" guy, and write me a note. He must be my "Phenomenon Guy" and buy all my chairs, meaning he must be interested in my passion for comforting children, and he can't need my money.'"

"Well then," Melody said, *"you're going to be single forever!"*

"That's what I'm counting on."

"And what money? Didn't you borrow from your mortgage payment this month to move, open your store, pay your rent, and everything else that you have going on. You don't have any money left."

"I know it seems crazy, but I prayed about this, and God clearly told me to go home and trust Him to provide what I need. I have to start over, and I chose to trust Him fully. At this point, I have nothing to lose except my faith, and that's one thing I'll never let go of! So, Melody, can we finally put the topic of finding my 'one true love' to rest?"

"Yes, Gina."

"Great Melody. I'll talk to you later." I clicked her off my Bluetooth and drove the rest of the way in silence and God's peace drove with me.

The following Monday, I woke up in a rented room, feeling like I was back at square one. I thought I had already experienced this fresh start in my 40s, but life had dealt me another new beginning in my 50s. This time, it felt different. I was in a small, borrowed space that wasn't my own. To be honest, I didn't jump out of bed with excitement. But when I realized I had nothing cool to wear, (the weather was in the 100s) I hastily got dressed in my jeans and headed to the last place I thought I'd ever miss — Kmart.

When I was done shopping, I thanked the cashier for her friendly service, grabbed my small purchase and when I turned to find the exit... that's when I saw Eldon Cyrus.

"Eldon, what are you doing sitting on this bench?" I asked with curiosity.

"Gina, what brings you to Grass Valley? Just visiting?" he replied.

"No, I actually moved back yesterday," I said, still settling into the thought myself.

We chatted for a few minutes before Eldon's eyes lit up. *"Hey, got a few minutes to spare? I'd love for you to follow me home and see what we've done with the livestock and equipment you gave us when you moved south."*

My mind flashed back to the prized goats, sows, farrowing crates, and farm gear I had handed over to Eldon's family before leaving for Southern California. It was a gesture to support their kids' 4-H endeavors and our local community. *"Absolutely, Eldon! I'd love to see the farm and how everything's come along."*

We drove off together, but Eldon quickly pulled ahead and turned right, instead of left. By the time I could turn, he was nowhere to be seen. I turned left, hoping he still lived in the same house I remembered, since right didn't seem like the correct direction. However, when I arrived, he was waiting for me with a warm smile. *"Hey, Gina! Over here! Come into the barn and take a look."*

We strolled around the farm for over an hour, Eldon proudly showing me the great-great grandkids of my former goats and sows. We entered the farrowing room, where my old equipment had found a new home, and he entertained me with stories of countless livestock births, 4-H ribbons won, and cherished family moments made possible by the gifts I had shared with him — gifts that had brought joy long after I could no longer tend to them myself.

As I prepared to leave, I turned to Eldon and said, *"Thank you so much for sharing this with me. Although my divorce from Glenn (and the loss of the life I loved) was difficult, seeing how you've created cherished moments with your family brings me joy. I'm forever grateful for our chance encounter today, which reminds me that life goes on when we're willing to share what we no longer need with those who can use it. It's a beautiful reminder that our stories can continue in new ways."*

"*Hey, Gina,*" Eldon said, as his voice softened. "*I have something for you. As I was leaving Kmart, God instructed me to give you a gift. I can't afford to part with it, but I can't ignore God's prompting either. So, please open your hand, and when I give this to you, promise me you won't try to return it.*"

"*Okay, I promise.*"

Eldon reached into his pocket, and I held out my hand, palm up. He placed a napkin in my hand, and I unfolded it. "*Eldon, what is this?*" I asked, my voice trembling.

"*It's exactly $620.00,*" he replied.

Tears sprang to my eyes as I realized the significance of the gift. I used the napkin to wipe away my tears, overwhelmed by God's appointment with the two of us. "*Eldon, no one but Melody knows this, but I've been waiting to move back to Grass Valley for over a year. The Lord told me it was time a few months ago, but unexpected expenses left me short $620.00 for my first month's expenses. I prayed, and the Lord promised to provide. I had to borrow from my mortgage payment, which is due to-morrow. God just used you to fulfill His promise to me!*"

Eldon and I sat down on a worn stump, tears streaming down our faces, and a profound silence surrounded us, and in that moment, we both knew that we would be okay. God had kept His promise to me, and Eldon's obedience had ensured His provision in a mighty way. We didn't need to say a word, because our hearts were filled with this unexplainable peace.

We never spoke of that moment again, but nine years later, as I sat at my computer writing about our divine appointment, I received a text that Eldon had passed away. On the very day I was writing this story, the Lord called him home, and I envisioned Jesus waiting at the gates of Heaven, smiling at Eldon with pride, saying, "*Well done, good and faithful servant. You have been faithful over a little; I will set you over much. Enter into the joy of your master.*" (Matthew 25:21)

"*For those who believe, no explanation is necessary. For those who do not be-lieve, no explanation is possible.*" — Franz Werfel

In memory of Eldon Lindsey Cyrus.

January 13, 1965 – June 8, 2024

Appointment Fifty-Two

"GOD, YOU HAVE 30 DAYS"

"Oh that I might have my request,
and that God would fulfill my hope."
Job 6:8

A few weeks after I had moved back to Northern California, I was getting ready to open a store for my non-profit, Owie BowWowie and Friends, with my good friend Steve Dowd. Steve was also gracious and rented me the upstairs of his house. I was very grateful to Steve for our friendship, but for also giving me a safe place to start over. Friendships are truly one of God's greatest blessings.

Then, as I was heading out the door to go to our store on Wednesday, I heard Steve yell, *"Hey Gina. Before you go to work would you mind paying a bill for me in Nevada City? This way I can do other things."* I grabbed his invoice, money, and out the door I went.

When I arrived in Nevada City it was a warm, cloudy, Wednesday day, and because the town was designed for miners in the 1800s, parking has always been a bit of a struggle, so I found myself parking on a hill that I needed to walk down, and as I was walking I heard God's voice say, *"Take a photo of that little white church."* So, I took a photo, thought nothing of it, and went about my business. But then after I had paid Steve's bill, I revisited my path only this time I was facing the little white church when I heard God's voice say, *"Now take another picture of the little white church.*" So, I took a photo, only this time I looked up to Heaven and said, *"Now, You have my attention."* And I left to go to work.

When I arrived at our store, I happened to look through the glass door and what I saw brought me great joy. There were gifts, and a few letters. I had written on Facebook that I had moved back to Nevada County and was going to open a store in July. I also shared where the store was located, and the day it would be opened, because I was anticipating a grand opening. What I wasn't expecting were gifts left behind my glass door. As I hurriedly opened the door, I picked up my pile of *"What could this be?"* and...

One by one I opened them until I got to a note that was written on a small yellow notepad that read...

"Hi Gina,

You might not remember me, but I remember going to a Bible study at your house with my brother, Dirk Meyer. I am Roland, and we have a mutual friend who said you might be interested in starting a Bible study, and guess what? My son, Roland is the pastor of First Baptist Church in Nevada City, and along with Sunday morning Bible studies we have an excellent study on Wednesday nights and potlucks, so I am inviting you, as you once invited me..."

His letter continued onward, but I stopped when I realized that just 20 minutes before reading his letter I had taken two photos of a little white church in Nevada City, so I put down the letter, reached for my phone and when I looked at the second photo there it read on the marquee, Pastor Roland Meyer, and my heart stopped!

As I read through the letter, and came upon the end, Roland had left his phone number so at 6pm that evening I called him and the two of us talked for two hours. When I told him about how God had me take two photos of his son's church that morning, he too couldn't believe it, and the two of us were in awe of how God works.

The following day was a Thursday, when I arrived at work and saw a tall, handsome, blue-eyed man, standing in front of my store holding two cups of coffee.

Two White Mocha's to be exact. I smiled, and the two of us became instant friends.

A week later, on a Wednesday, I was in my store, placing items on my shelves when Roland walked in with a case filled with honey, *"What is this?"* I asked.

"I thought you might like to sell honey in your store, so I bought you this case of honey to sell." He replied.

"That is so sweet of you, but I can't sell honey in my store. I'm not licensed to sell food."

"Well then, how much do you want for your honey?" he asked.

"What do you mean? That's not my honey. It's your honey. You bought it."

"No, I brought you the honey so you could sell the honey and if you can't sell the honey to other people then I will buy the honey from you."

The two of us went back and forth on the honey for what seemed like forever until finally he frustratedly said, *"Look, I'm not leaving here today unless I buy all of your honey so how much do you want for your honey?"*

"Okay, fine! How about a quarter for all the honey?"

Without saying another word, he reached into his pocket, pulled out a hundred-dollar bill, placed it on my counter, grabbed his honey and off he went.

Another 22 days went by and the two of us had become inseparable. It seemed that from the moment he handed me my White Mocha we had become the best of friends, and on this Sunday, we had just finished up with church, and I was in my car getting ready to head home when all of a sudden Roland walked up to my car window, reached into his pocket, pulled out an envelope, reached through my car door window and handing me an envelope he said, *"Please don't open this until I'm gone."*

When he pulled away, I quickly opened it and inside was a letter that read, *"My sweet Gina, God put it on my heart to give this to you today. I know how hard it is to start over again and I need you to know that I don't need your money."* Then I looked into the envelope, and he had placed two, one-hundred-dollar bills inside.

As I sat in front of the little white church, I heard God's voice say, *"I heard you when you said, 'Okay, Mel, this is what I'm going to do. I'm going to ask God this.*

God, if you want me to be with someone you have 30 days to bring him to me. And, he must be my "Notebook" guy, and write me a note. He must be my "Phenomenon Guy" and buy all my chairs, meaning he must be interested in my passion for comforting children, and he can't need my money."'

OH MY GOSH! I thought. God did it! In less than 30 days He brought me my notebook guy, because Roland left me a note. He brought me my Phenomenon guy, because while I didn't have a store filled with chairs like the movie, he bought all the honey. And he brought me a guy that didn't value me off of what I earned, but by whom God had created me to be!

When I had come to the realization that God had answered my prayer that I prayed in anger I couldn't believe it, because while I said to Melody that I never wanted to get married again, the truth-of-the-matter was, I did. I wanted someone who would write me love notes, buy whatever I had to sell, and love me when I had nothing left to give.

The best part of my appointment with God, was shortly after I told Roland about my prayer in anger, and how God had sent him to me, he told me that shortly before I arrived back in town he had prayed. He had asked the Lord to either bring him a Christian woman whom he could love for the rest of his days or take away the loneliness that he had felt when he was alone. He wanted peace from whatever God had decided to give him, and because both of us had asked God to bring us what we needed...

We were a match made from Heaven.

On December 21, 2016, (on the longest night of the year) the two of us drove up to Downieville, California, and under the gallows, with wedding rings made from the ends of two shotgun barrels, we got married. And we did this as a reminder that... "till death do us part."

And we lived happily ever after.

When Gina Woods became Gina Meyer

Appointment Fifty-Three

"MARCH"

"And He said to them, 'Pay attention to what you hear:
with the measure you use, it will be measured to you,
and still more will be added to you.'"

Mark 4:24

It was a cold and rainy Wednesday afternoon when I was working in my office, and for whatever reason I didn't like the silence. I needed noise. So, I turned on the television and got back to work. I wasn't listening to what was being said until I heard this question posed, *"Who has been praying for you not to get pregnant?"*

I had it turned to one of the Christian television stations and a pastor happened to be telling a story about a woman who came up to him after church and she asked, *"Pastor, will you pray for me because I can't get pregnant?"* And that's when he responded, *"Who has been praying for you not to get pregnant?"*

At that moment I stopped working and listened.

He continued onward with his story...

"What do you mean?" she asked him. *"No one would ever pray for that."*

A moment later he heard a woman's voice say from behind her, *"No. You're wrong. I have been praying that over you because you're my daughter and have never been that healthy and I didn't want to lose my daughter by giving birth, so I have been praying for you not to get pregnant."*

As I listened to the rest of the story I began to sob, because my youngest daughter, Shae, was trying to get pregnant and she couldn't so at that moment I bowed my head and through my tears I said, *"God, I'm so sorry. I too have been praying that Shae wouldn't get pregnant. She isn't that healthy, and I've been so worried that I would lose her giving birth to a baby and I didn't want to lose my baby. I've been so selfish to worry and I'm so sorry."*

A moment later I heard God's voice say, *"Call Shae at work and ask her if she still wants to get pregnant, what she wants, and ask her if she has a name picked out."*

I immediately called her at work, *"Mom, is everything okay?"*

"Yes, why?" I asked.

"Because we're both working, and you only call me at work if there's an emergency."

"Oh, no. I'm fine. I just want to know if you want to get pregnant, do you want a boy or a girl and if so, have you picked out a name?"

"Mom, this is a weird phone call."

"I know, I don't have time to explain the whole story, but God wanted me to call you and ask you, so please just answer my questions."

Then within a quiet whisper she said, *"Yes. We want to have a child. We want a boy, and we'd like to name him Cash James."*

"Like Cash after Johnny Cash?" I asked.

"Yes."

"Okay, that's all I need to know."

The two of us hung up the phone, I grabbed a piece of paper and in blue ink I wrote Pray for Cash James, and then I heard God say, *"Add March,"* so I added the month of March. I then found a tack and placed the note on my bulletin board and went about my business.

Then a few months went by, and Shae flew out to visit me from Chicago. The two of us were in my office when she happened to look up and asked, *"Mom, what's that?"*

"Oh, remember the day I called you and asked you if you wanted to have a child?"

"Yes."

"That's your baby. You're going to get pregnant, and he will be a boy named Cash James. God told me."

Shae gave me a look of sarcasm and then asked, "What's the March for?"

"Oh, I don't know. Maybe you will get pregnant in March, he'll be born in March, I don't know. All I know is God told me to write that month down so I did and there it will stay."

"Mom, I love you, but I've been trying to get pregnant for a long time so please don't be disappointed when it doesn't happen this way."

"Oh, it will happen. God told me."

And there we left it.

Shae went home and a few months went by and one Saturday morning my phone rang, and it was Shae, "Mom, are you sitting down. I have something I want to tell you."

"Yes, I'm sitting down and you're pregnant!"

"YES!!! You were right about my being pregnant, but March doesn't make any sense. Anyway, I'm still excited! I'M PREGNANT!"

We celebrated this joyous occasion for weeks, until one afternoon.

It was a Wednesday, when Shae called me in tears. She had just gone to the doctor's and had received news that she had lost her baby in utero and had to have a D&C. We were all devastated and I was angry. I couldn't believe that God would tell me that she was going to have a baby, and then take the baby home, so that evening, I went into my garden and planted a mustard seed. Then each morning thereafter I would go to where my seed was, water it and watch it grow. Day after day I prayed that God would fulfill His promise, and then one afternoon I walked out and my mustard seed had grown into a beautiful, yellow bush of flowers and it was then when my phone rang and I noticed it was Shae so I answered and heard, "Mom, I didn't want to tell you, because I didn't want to get my hopes up, but I'm pregnant.

I've been pregnant for a few months, and they did an ultrasound today and the baby is doing well. They took a blood test to see if they can tell the sex of the baby, but my doctor said it still may be too soon."

I couldn't believe it because when Shae called me it was March 30th, and that is when Shae said, *"I know what you're thinking mom. It's March, but I didn't find out I was pregnant in March and the baby won't be born in March, so it doesn't count that I am telling you in March. The doctor said even if they can tell the sex of the baby, I just took the test, and they won't get the results back until next week, so the whole March thing won't work. It would be cool if they could, but it won't happen, so I don't want you to get your hopes up!"* My hopes were up, because I knew God would fulfill His promise.

March 31st was a Wednesday, when my phone rang, *"Mom, you're not going to believe this."*

"You've got the results of the sex?"

"Yes! Nick is on his way to go pick them up. They were going to tell me over the phone, but I wanted Nick and I to be together. I'll call you back."

There was really no need for her to call me back. I knew that her baby was going to be a boy, and that is why God had me write down March. Of course, He knew that Shae wouldn't be able to keep her first son, Cash James. For whatever reason God had, He gave her a gift of naming her son, Cash James, and one day... many years from now, she will meet him face-to-face. God also knew that Shae was only going to have one child, and she wanted a son, so I knew that her child would be a boy, I just didn't know his name.

A few hours later my phone rang again, and it was Shae, *"Mom..."*

"I know. It's a boy."

"YES! It's a boy and we found out on the last day of March! A little creepy and cool all at the same time." She said.

I hung up the phone, got down on my knees and thanked God for the blessing that our family had received because there are no accidents with God. Only appointments.

And, looking back on my life I find it very interesting that God allowed me to have a dream when Cadynce, my first grandchild was born, and He told me the month of when my last grandson would be introduced into the world.

On October 13, 2021, Donnie James was born into the world, and one day I will tell him the story of how he has a brother who lives in Heaven and how God gave us him so that we all could "March" onward by faith!

Appointment Fifty-Four

"A LEGACY PRESERVED"

""Lord, remember me when You come into Your Kingdom."
Luke 23:42

July 16, 2024, was a Wednesday morning when my sister, Ann Strum, called and told me she was in remission, and I cried tears of relief.

I cried because this wasn't the first time she went through cancer. Years back she was diagnosed with breast cancer, and had to endure chemo, radiation, and a double mastectomy. Then in January of 2023, she was diagnosed with esophageal cancer and had to go through Keytruda, chemo, radiation and is continuing her treatment with Keytruda, (which is an immunotherapy and works with the immune system to fight off cancer cells). Her body responded to Keytruda in a positive way, and that is the reason she is in remission today.

I also cried because it was a blessing to know that I wasn't going to lose her, too.

On Wednesday, December 29th, 2021, we lost our brother Matt Strum. He died shortly after his 50th birthday due to liver and kidney failure caused from drinking. Our brother was an alcoholic and so was my sister. The only difference was a few years prior to my brother's death, and after my sister survived her breast cancer, she put herself into rehab, worked very hard and came out sober. I was so angry when my brother died, because when his liver and kidney failed him, and he had to be placed in the hospital, that was when he wanted to sober up. His plan was to get out of the hospital, go to rehab, find a great group of people in AA, and live his happily ever after, but that wasn't possible for him. On Christmas Eve, just a few short days from when the Lord called him home, I was sitting in church and my sister called to tell me that while he was getting dialysis, he had had a stroke and he wanted to talk to me. I told him I loved him; and through an unrecognizable voice, he told me he loved me more, and on Christmas morning I flew to be with him.

My family and I spent every moment with him in the hospital until he passed, but the night before he left us, my mother asked me if he ever decided to believe in Jesus.

"*Well, mom.*" I replied. "*Months before Matt came to the hospital, he would fall asleep at night watching a movie on HBO but when he'd wake up the channel had somehow miraculously changed, and a woman named Joyce Meyer would be talking. One day he called me and asked if I knew who she was. When I told him I did, he said, 'she reminds me of the way you talk about Jesus. Maybe I'll listen to her.' Then one day he texted me: 'Joyce is on,' and he kept texting me every time he watched her ministry: Joyce is on. This was his way of letting me that that he was listening. Then on December 10, he sent me this text.*" Then reaching my phone to where my mother could see it, I read Matt's text to her, "*I told Jesus today that He could watch over me and I would do the rest.*"

My brother died a few short hours after he rested, and I knew that Jesus would watch over him from that day onward.

Then in August of 2022, I was in Chicago visiting my daughter, Shae, when I received a phone call from a hospital in Southern California. Not knowing the number, I declined the call because I thought it had to be a wrong number, but when the number called back, I picked it up, "*Hello, Gina.*"

"*Yes.*"

"*This is Richie, your father. I wanted to let you know that I'm in the hospital. My legs gave out a few days ago and I had to call the ambulance to help me. A few moments ago, the doctor came in and told me that I have stage 4 prostate cancer and must have back surgery. I just wanted you to know in case something happens to me, that I'm sorry we missed so many decades, but I loved that we reconnected and were able to see each other again."*

In the past 46 years I had only seen him once. I had talked to him on the phone several times, but I never drove back to visit him, and here we were. We were right back to the day where he handed me the Cinderella watch and drove away, only this time it might not be a car that takes him away from me again, but a chariot, and I said, *"I'll see you soon."*

When I returned from Chicago, I headed to Southern California, where fate brought us together once again. This time, as I saw him, I understood the divine appointment that had led to reunite us. I am my father's last living relative, and had we not reconnected, his legacy would have been lost forever. There would have been no one to open the doors to his home, discover the treasure trove of over 2,000 books and notebooks filled with his thoughts and reflections, and carry on his passion for storytelling. But now, I had the privilege of building his library, a testament to his life's journey, and keeping his memory alive. Our reunion was not just a coincidence, but a divine appointment with God to preserve his legacy and continue onward with his story.

If we hadn't reconnected, someone else would have opened the door to his home, but they would have found only meaningless relics — over 2,000 books and notebooks filled with his thoughts and reflections. They would have discarded his life's work, erasing his legacy, and my father's existence would have been reduced to nothing more than a faint memory. His story, his passions, and his heart would have been lost forever, leaving behind only a faint whisper of a life once lived. But because we reconnected, I was able to preserve his legacy, and his memory lives on through me.

They say that you die three times; The first is when the body ceases to function. The second is when the body enters the grave. The third is that moment, sometime in our future, when your name is spoken for the last time.

My Final Appointment

"IT IS FINISHED!"

"I shall not die, but I shall live,
and recount the deeds of the LORD."
Psalm 118: 17

As I stood in front of the rusted gate and dilapidated headstone in deep reflection of my past 61 years of life, I noticed the sun was beginning to fade, and the cherubim was still waiting for me to make my final decision, and right as I was getting ready to reflect on another past moment of my life, I heard…

"Gina, you have run out of time to decide…

If you believe that I Am who I say I Am, then you will stretch out your right hand and place it on the trunk of your tree and every story of your life will be recorded within the tree and your name will be added within the Book of Life. If you do not believe that I Am who I say I Am, then you will stretch out your left hand and place it on the trunk of the tree and My cherubim will cut down your tree and burn it. Your life will be as if you never existed. Do you understand?"

"Yes, I understand!"

"Do you believe that I Am who I say I Am?"

The question hung in the air, heavy with anticipation. With a sense of surrender, I pushed open the creaky gate, its rusted hinges groaning in protest. I closed it softly behind me, as if sealing my fate. Then, with deliberate steps, I approached the weathered headstone, its inscription still legible despite the passage of time. The words, once bold and proud, now seemed to whisper a gentle affirmation, as if echoing the question that still lingered in my heart...

Born with Wisdom — Died with Grace

Then with a gentle gesture, I raised my right hand and placed it upon the tree. In an instant, the Dogwood Tree vanished, replaced by a book that seemed to materialize from the very essence of the moment. As I looked around, I noticed the cherubim was gone, leaving behind a comforting stillness. The silence was profound, a symphony of peace that caught me in its gentle embrace. The world seemed to hold its breath, as if waiting for me to open the book and unlock the secrets within.

As I reached down to pick up the book of my life, I heard...

"Now, I ask you to focus your heart and mind on the truth I'm about to reveal. The memories that linger, the ones that shaped your life as you reflected on your journey, were the legacies I orchestrated through others. A legacy is the lasting impact of a moment, a decision, or an encounter that forever changes the trajectory of one's life. The people I brought into your life, those I took away, and those who remain by your side today — each one left an indelible mark on your soul. They contributed to the person you are today, and their influence is a testament to their faithfulness. Every appointment, every encounter, was a divine assignment, a sacred trust. These individuals were faithful servants, delivering the messages I intended for you to receive. They showed up at our appointed times, and their presence altered the course of your life. Embrace the truth: you are the culmination of these legacies, and their impact will continue to unfold as long as you continue to share their stories."

And remember... It is His wonderful life that gave you your wonderful life.

IT IS FINISHED!

EPILOGUE

"Oil and perfume make the heart glad, and the sweetness of a friend comes from his earnest counsel." Proverbs 27:9

After completing *Appointments With God*, I shared my manuscript with a few trusted friends, including Gary Stuhlmiller. As writers know, it takes courage to share our work and hear feedback. On Tuesday, August 6, 2024, Gary called, asking if I was ready to hear his thoughts. I hesitated, but said, *"Yes, please, give it to me straight."* Gary shared his insights, then asked, *"Gina, where's the Appointment With God about the day at the church?"* I had forgotten about it, having shared many of these divine encounters verbally, still reeling from their impact. *"You mean the day God was upset with me?"* I clarified. *"Yes, that one,"* Gary replied. *"It needs to be included."* As Gary spoke, I realized the value of sharing our stories with others before writing them down. We can forget the amazing things God does for us, and sometimes we don't want to remember when God scolds us. But friends like Gary remind us of the moments God never wants us to forget. Thank you, Gary, for showing me that sharing our stories, even the difficult ones, can bring glory to God and inspire others

It was a Tuesday morning, December 18, 2018, to be exact when I was opening the church door to enter, and as I was opening the door I was talking to my daughter, Heidi on the phone. *"Hold on a moment Heidi. I want to hear what you have to say, but the key isn't cooperating."* I placed my phone on the ground, opened the door, and as I went to put the receiver back up to my ear, I heard this loud voice say, *"GINA! GINA!"*

"MOM! Who just yelled your name?" Heidi asked.

"I don't know."

"Hello!" I yelled towards the stairs. *"Who's up there?"*

Silence fell over the church and creeping halfway up the stairs I said again,

"Hello. Who just called my name?"

"Mom, is anyone up there?"

"I don't know. I'm too afraid to walk all the way up and look. I'm the only one who is supposed to be here today."

"Mom, get out of there, now."

I ran down the stairs and out the door I went, *"Heidi. Let me call you back. I want to call Pastor Roland* (who is my husband's son) *and see if he's here. Hiding somewhere."*

"Hello! What's up, Gina?" Pastor Roland asked as he picked up my call.

"Hey, are you here? Someone just yelled my name twice from upstairs. Are you playing a joke or something because it's not funny."

"No, Gina. I would never do that to you. I'm at a pastor's meeting. No one else is supposed to be there today. Call my dad and have him come check it out."

"Good idea."

Within a minute I called my husband, and he agreed to come and check it out, but then I thought to myself, what if my mind was hearing things? But then how would Heidi hear it, too?

At that moment my phone rang, and it was Heidi, *"Mom, was it Roland? Was he playing a joke on you?"*

"No, he's at a meeting. This is silly. Maybe we just heard the wind blow or something. I'm going back in."

"Mom, please don't go back in that church. I heard what I heard."

"Stay on the phone with me. I'm going."

I then took a deep breath, opened the front door and the minute I stepped foot into the foyer, I heard, *"GINA! GINA!"*

"MOM, what the heck? I heard that voice call your name again, only this time it sounded close. Where was that coming from?"

I froze and whispered, *"The voice is coming from downstairs and now it's in the church."*

"Mom, please get out of there. PLEASE!"

I then walked slowly towards the foyer doors, and pushed one open, *"Hello. Who's down here?"*

I heard and saw nothing, so I quickly ran out of the church and waited for my husband to arrive, and when he did the two of us walked through and around the church and heard nothing.

"Roland, who was calling my voice?" I asked inquisitively.

"The Lord was calling you." He replied.

"What do you mean the Lord was calling me?"

"Gina, you know. The story of Samuel." He then walked over to one of the pews, picked up the Bible and read: *"The boy Samuel ministered before the* LORD *under Eli. In those days the word of the* LORD *was rare; there were not many visions. One night Eli, whose eyes were becoming so weak that he could barely see, was lying down in his usual place. The lamp of God had not yet gone out, and Samuel was lying down in the house of the Lord, where the ark of God was. Then the* LORD *called Samuel. Samuel answered, 'Here I am.' And he ran to Eli and said, 'Here I am; you called me.' But Eli said, 'I did not call; go back and lie down.' So he went and lay down. Again the* LORD *called, 'Samuel!' And Samuel got up and went to Eli and said, 'Here I am; you called me.' 'My son,' Eli said, 'I did not call; go back and lie down.' Now Samuel did not yet know the* LORD*: The word of the* LORD *had not yet been revealed to him. A third time the* LORD *called, 'Samuel!' And Samuel got up and went to Eli and said, 'Here I am; you called me.' Then Eli realized that the* LORD *was calling the boy. So Eli told Samuel, 'Go and lie down, and if He calls you, say, "Speak,* LORD, *for Your servant is listening."' So Samuel went and lay down in his place. The* LORD *came and stood there, calling as at the other times, 'Samuel! Samuel!' Then Samuel said, 'Speak, for Your servant is listening.'"* 1 Samuel 3:1-10

I didn't know what to say.

When the two of us got home, Pastor Roland called and said for my husband and me to meet him back at the church the following morning. He had called two other women who had attended our church, Kris Cyrus and Lynn Salmoria, because the two of them were mighty prayer warriors, and he thought it might help to put my heart at ease that if it was God talking I might be able to hear Him again, and if it wasn't... we could pray away the voice that Heidi and I had heard.

On December 19, 2018, a Wednesday, our group gathered inside the church, seeking divine guidance. As they prayed, Lynn stood up and asked, *"Father, if it's Your voice calling Gina, please reveal Yourself to her."* In that moment, a faint fog appeared beside her, visible only to my eyes. A gentle whisper spoke directly to my heart, saying, *"LET THE TRUTH REVEAL THE TRUTH! I called you to come to Me, but you ran. I had to come down to you, and still, you ran again. You didn't trust the voice that's guided you your whole life. I even allowed our Heidi to hear My voice, to be My witness, but you both ran. I'm disappointed, Gina. You're so busy, yet you're not completing the work I've assigned to you. You don't know how much time you have left, but you keep running from the work I'm doing through you. Fearful of others' opinions, you're missing out on the greatest moments of your life. I've shown you the way through dreams, conversations, and the people I've sent to you. Still, you run. That's the problem — everyone runs from the truth, missing Me in the process. Now, listen carefully. I want you to write the stories I tell you, without fear of judgment. These stories are to bless those I've had you write about, showcasing their faithfulness and the legacy they've left with you. The ending of your story marks the beginning for My readers, where they can choose to make an appointment with Me. Understand, Gina, that you must finish what I started, for I who began a good work in you will bring it to completion on the day of Jesus Christ, as promised in Philippians 1:6. Now, go and finish!"*

As the voice faded, the faint fog vanished, leaving me breathless and tearful. I gazed around at the group, my eyes overflowing with uncontrollable tears, and whispered, *"It was God's voice... He's angry with me."* Overwhelmed, I fled the church, seeking solace in my car. But God's gentle whisper followed me, *"Stop and get a notebook, write down what you hear."* I obeyed, driving 45 minutes to Barnes and Noble, searching for the per-

fect notebook. As I wandered through the aisles, I stumbled, accidentally bumping a bookshelf, and a notebook fell to the ground. But I knew it was no accident — it was another divine Appointment With God. I picked up the notebook, feeling an inexplicable sense of purpose, and knew that this was the beginning of a sacred journey. I would record the whispers of God and finish the good work that God had begun in me. The *Appointments With God* that you've read were the stories He wanted me to share with you, His reader, with the hope that you'll understand: disappointments in life are nothing more than *Appointments With God*.

PLEASE MEET MY FRIEND, GARY STUHLMILLER...

It was sometime in early 2008 when Gina and I became connected as friends on FaceBook. Through our first few chats, we quickly appreciated the large number of mutual interests, likes and dislikes, such as Christmas being a year-round celebration, and the love of our Lord Jesus Christ. To me, it felt as though I had gained a sister, and routinely refer to her as "Sis" in chats or telephone calls. In October of that year, we had the opportunity to meet in person while I was in Los Angeles to attend a conference. Over lunch at a classic 1960's burger restaurant, we shared a great many of our experiences; most of our time centered around how we had each sensed God speaking to our hearts. I learned about many of Gina's *Appointments With God*, some of which she has already shared with you in this book; others were yet to be experienced. And I shared with her my own experience in hearing, not just sensing, but hearing God speaking directly to me.

My story begins with my having experienced a painful divorce, one in which, by worldly standards, I felt I had been unjustly treated. My first step toward healing came with making the decision to forgive, completely, all the perceived offenses I had endured. The next step was God's. Divorce involves loss, loss of family, children, friends, finances... One evening, I was kneeling in prayer about my plight, feeling very sorry for myself, crying out to God in my misery, when from behind my right shoulder came a voice — *"Seek ye first the Kingdom of God and His righ-*

teousness, and all these things shall be added unto you." (Matthew 7:33) I quickly turned around to see who had come into my room but there was no one to be seen. From that moment forward, and still today, my life changed. I had heard God speaking directly to me in my need; He had given me His promise, and my call to serve Him began.

Perhaps this is why Gina called me the day after she heard God calling her in the church. She knew I would understand who had called to her, and that I would encourage her to fulfill the mission to which God was calling her. God had given Gina a beautiful gift of creative writing and He intended that she use it to His praise and glory. Through the years since that conversation, Gina and I have often spoken about her book, she sometimes telling me about new appointments she had experienced and me encouraging her to finish the book. In the fullness of time, Gina sent me the draft of her manuscript to read, review, proof, and edit. Her (God's) timing could not have been more perfect from my perspective.

As I read through each of the 54 appointments, I came to appreciate how beautifully her book could tie in with the text of a homily I was preparing for worship that next Sunday at Grace Lutheran Church in Durham, NC. The text for the homily is taken from I Kings 19:1-8. It is part of the narrative concerning the prophet, Elijah, and his ministry at the time when King Ahab and Queen Jezebel ruled in Israel. The full narrative is found in I Kings chapters 18 and 19, and is among my favorite biblical narratives, one well worth your time to read. Verses 1-8 of Chapter 19 relate Elijah's flight from Queen Jezebel and his feeding by an angel as he flees. Elijah had experienced God's awesome power in several ways prior to this flight. He had been fed in the wilderness by food brought to him by ravens; he had raised a widow's son from death; he had huge victory over 450 prophets of Baal on Mt. Carmel, and he had outrun Ahab's chariot back to the capital city, Jezreel. And now, because Jezebel threatened to kill him, he ran in fear for his life. But, as he will soon learn, he was actually running to his appointment with God. As was true for Gina, God still had work for Elijah to do. And so, while Elijah was hiding in a cave, God spoke to him: *"Elijah, what are you doing here?"* God told Elijah to stand at the mouth of the cave, and that God was about to pass by. First came powerful wind; next came a powerful earthquake and then raging fire, but God was not in the wind, nor the earthquake, nor the fire. Lastly came a still, small voice, a voice that repeated the question, *"Elijah, what are you doing here?"* And with that came God's assurance that Elijah was not the only one in Israel who had not bowed his knee to Baal, and God sent Elijah off to complete the work he was intended to accomplish.

In thinking about my upcoming homily about this passage, I am reminded, through the revelation of the Holy Spirit, of the many others in the Bible who experienced "appointments with God" — Adam and Eve in the Garden of Eden, Noah being told to build the Ark, Abram whose name was changed to Abraham, and who became the father of many nations, Jacob, who wrestled with God and came out of it with a dislocated hip and a new name — Israel, Moses whose appointments with God spanned 40 years — Samuel, Isaiah, Job, and of course, everyone who had interaction with our Lord Jesus Christ.

And now we come to you, the reader of this book. I hope this book was a wonderful blessing in your life — that you can now reflect back on your life and now appreciate many times that were your own appointments with God. If you can do so, it is because our loving God has revealed these to you. Sometimes, He speaks to us in a still, small voice within our spirit; sometimes He speaks to us aloud.

"For it is by grace you have been saved, through faith — and this is not from yourselves, it is the gift of God —not by works, so that no one can boast. For we are God's workmanship, created in Jesus Christ to do good works, which God prepared in advance for us to do." Ephesians 2:8-10

God still has work for you to do in His kingdom. And so, as God once asked Elijah, *"What are you doing here Elijah?"* I now ask you, what are YOU doing here?

NOW, IT'S TIME FOR YOU
TO MAKE A DECISION.

Dear Reader! Listen carefully. The tree that you see on this page is yours. If you believe that I Am who I say I Am, then you will stretch out your right hand and place it on the trunk of your tree and every story of your life will be recorded within the tree and your name will be added within the Book of Life. *"And I saw the dead, great and small, standing before the throne, and books were opened. Then another book was opened, which is the Book of Life."* Revelation 20:12

If you do not believe that I Am who I say I Am, then you will stretch out your left hand and place it on the trunk of the tree and your tree will be cut down and burned. Your life will be as if you never existed. *"And if anyone's name was not found written in the Book of Life, he was thrown into the lake of fire."* Revelation 20:15

You see, you are the only person who can make this decision for you. Choose wisely.

Love,
God

"Hope deferred makes the heart sick,
but a longing fulfilled is a Tree of Life."
Proverbs 13:12

f @onwardbyfaith *and* @appointmentswithgod

⊙ @onwardbyfaith

www.onwardbyfaith.com

A HEARTFELT REQUEST

(FROM THE PUBLISHERS)

I still remember the day my daughter Heidi, then just eight years old, said with excitement, *"Mom, one day I'm going to be so famous that everyone will sign my autograph book!"* Her enthusiasm was infectious, and I promised myself that one day I would be that famous, too.

Now, Deborah and I are thrilled to invite you to be a part of our own autograph book journey! We'd be honored if you would sign your name and join the community of those who have supported us along the way. To make it easy, simply:

1. Tear out this page.
2. Sign your name with a personal message (if desired).
3. Mail it to:

Onward by Faith Publishing
PO Box 1527
Cedar Ridge, CA 95924

We'll treasure your signature and add it to our *Onward by Faith* autograph book, a keepsake that will inspire us for years to come. Thank you for being part of our journey!

Please turn page and sign on back.

Signature:

Message:

www.ingramcontent.com/pod-product-compliance
Lightning Source LLC
Chambersburg PA
CBHW060136130626

46556CB00006B/2375